GREEK
MYTHOLOGY

ΕΚΔΟΣΕΙΣ
TEXNH
EDITIONS

"The Island of the Sirens" a wood-carving by the Greek painter and engraver K. Grammatopoulos.

© Copyright 1998   TECHNI S.A.
Nisiza Karela, Koropi, Attiki.
Telephone: +30 210 6028933, Fax: +30 210 6640205
Web Site: http://www.toubis.gr

ISBN: 960-540-266-1

TABLE OF CONTENTS

An introduction to

Intellect is the gift of the human race, the greatest and most enduring of all time.
This is the means by which it perceives, exists, creates and evolves.
No matter how extensive knowledge is, it has its limits.
Intellect thirsts for fulfillment, to ceaselessly push these limits outward.
Thus, people in that far-off period wanted to learn for they felt powerless and
vulnerable in a world without bounds. They were deeply concerned with the
beginning and the end and all the supernatural forces that could not be
mastered. Through intellect, humanity came to fashion its view of the world.
Utilizing the raw information from its immediate surroundings,
it cultivated knowledge and experience, while imagination filled in the rest.
Mankind had need of "Myth" because that was his own personal truth.
His faith in this increased his certitude about the world he had created around
himself. This is how we have come to accept the myth.
In its conventional sense, that is, a narration that informs us
about an older order of the world and explains it.
The content of Greek mythology is not a simple matter.
There is a practically endless series of accounts from various periods,
and derivations on which enormous an classificatory endeavor
has been expended and that is only the beginning.
Even more research was required to cross-reference and parallel mythical
and/or historical events and narrations in order to validate them.
This may seem strange, but Greek myth is not entirely a "fairy tale".
It is a representation of certain far-off periods and helps fill in the gaps in
history, but above all else it indicates the level that a culture had achieved.
Manners and customs, religion and the superstitions of a people
that had a historical presence for thousands of years before,
is not a "myth" in any sense. Because, though the gods and the incredible

Greek Mythology

encounters of the heroes with supernatural beings may have been the creations of fantasy, they arose from a fundamental truth that told one then, and tells one now, that a certain number of people in this corner of the world, many centuries before the advent of Christ, were building cities, subduing natural forces and foreign nations, setting off to unknown parts, founding colonies, leading art to great heights and cultivating the body and the spirit. All this was being done by the Greeks alone! When one speaks of the Cyclopian walls of the Mycenaean period, one immediately understands that the myth came to exist because the work was such a superhuman achievement for that period; it seemed these walls could have only been created by giants such as the Cyclopses. The stirring narrations of Homer are not merely the product of a cultural heritage and the imagination of people who lived three thousand years before. Let us never forget how the world was left speechless when the excavations at Troy and Mycenae brought to light proof of his account of their cultural magnificence, the wars they fought and the heroes who fought them, all before 1200 B.C.! The Troy of Priam emerged with its walls and its sanctuaries, while the "rich in gold Mycenaeans" as Homer refers to them, and the tombs of Atreas and Agamemnon, also laden with gold, came to light. The word mythology is Greek and has been adopted by other languages, sharing the universal values of this wealth that has survived right down to the present. This golden heritage of Homer, Hesiod, the great tragic and lyric writers of antiquity, as well as so many others from that period, is the pride of the Greek people. Because without this, European education as we know it would not exist; without this, worldwide literature would today be a much poorer thing.

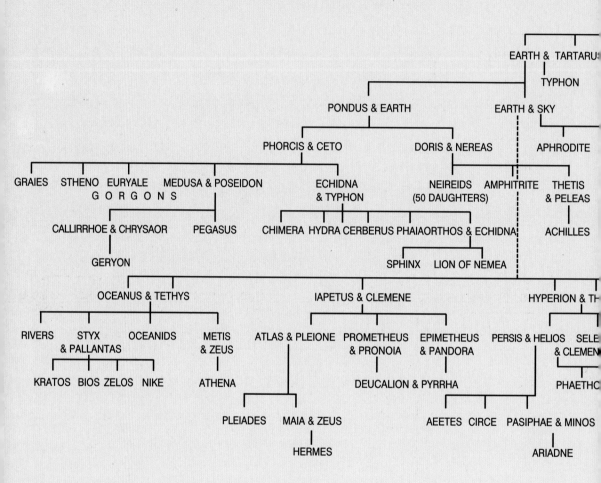

The Titans, gods and heroes of Greek mythology
are all branches of the same family tree.
The elements, divine races and gods gave birth to the great
champions of the myths. Nothing happens by chance,
everything has a reason and a purpose. Monsters are created
to punish the disrespectful and the morally offensive,
and alongside them the heroes arise who are praised
for defeating them. Above all, it is the gods who determine
the destiny of mankind.

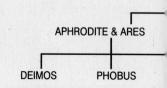

ds & Heroes

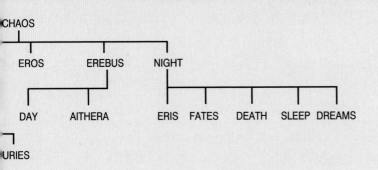

CHAOS

EROS · EREBUS · NIGHT

DAY · AITHERA · ERIS · FATES · DEATH · SLEEP · DREAMS

URIES

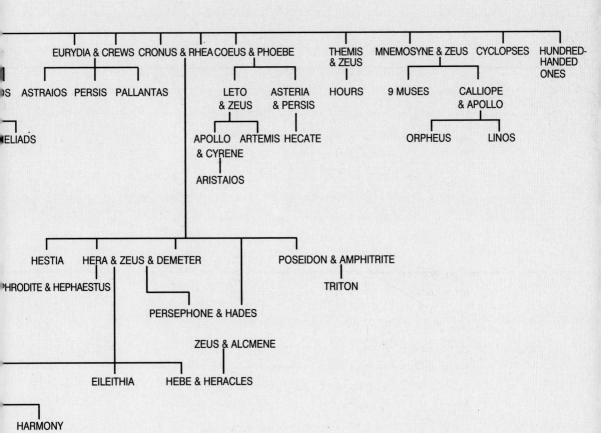

EURYDIA & CREWS · CRONUS & RHEA · COEUS & PHOEBE · THEMIS & ZEUS · MNEMOSYNE & ZEUS · CYCLOPSES · HUNDRED-HANDED ONES

OS · ASTRAIOS · PERSIS · PALLANTAS · LETO & ZEUS · ASTERIA & PERSIS · HOURS · 9 MUSES · CALLIOPE & APOLLO

ELIADS · APOLLO & CYRENE · ARTEMIS · HECATE · ORPHEUS · LINOS

ARISTAIOS

HESTIA · HERA & ZEUS & DEMETER · POSEIDON & AMPHITRITE

PHRODITE & HEPHAESTUS · TRITON

PERSEPHONE & HADES

ZEUS & ALCMENE

EILEITHIA · HEBE & HERACLES

HARMONY

Chapter 1

Creation of the Gods

*T*he ancient Greeks with their brilliant and imaginative
spirit created a complete order of things that functioned
harmoniously in the infinite world that contained them.
The beginning and the genesis of this world occupied them
in the same way it did the early people of every civilization.
Thus, they interpreted natural forces and unexplained
phenomena in what they considered a reasonable way,
true to a system of laws which arose from a respect for the
superior beings who defined and ruled the universe.
The stimuli from the environment and the incredible vastness
they saw around them made these early people, in what is
now called Greece, deify abstract concepts, elements of nature
and all the other amazing things they believed regulated
their fortunes and their survival.
But the divinity that was worshipped above all others
during prehistoric times (and not only in Greece but among
nearly all peoples) was Mother Earth.
Those far-off people trod the surface of the earth and were
nourished by its fruits. For Mediterranean people, Mother
Earth was frequently identified with the goddess of fertility;
the first idols from that period, also found in Greece,
depict this female figure with naked, full breasts
and a disproprotionately large pelvis, a typical sign
of fertility. The cultivation of the earth was clearly
connected to religious practices.

A knowledge of these early gods will reveal that they evolved along with Greek thought. The sceptre of the lords of the world changed hands until the most powerful came to dominate. The battles of the Titans and the Giants gave rise to a new generation of gods who then gained control. Together with these gods, the human race took its first halting steps and right from the very start paid the price for its weakness, even though its fate had already been determined by these very gods.

Starting with the first gods and goddesses, one arrives at those that prevailed and that are better known. The names of some of them will be mentioned only because the great protagonists of the following chapters came from them: the Greek gods and heroes.

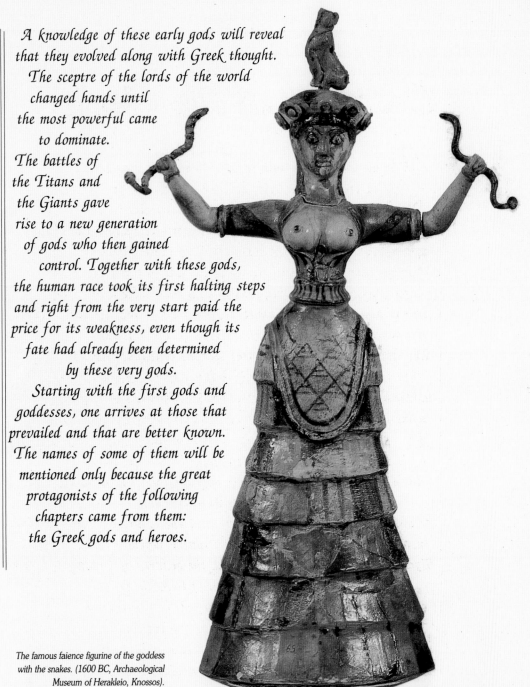

The famous faience figurine of the goddess with the snakes. (1600 BC, Archaeological Museum of Herakleio, Knossos).

THE FIRST GODS

E very tale and every truth involved with the creation of the universe has always begun with Chaos. Therefore, Chaos was also deified in the birth of the ancient Greek world. Erebus and Night were originally born of Chaos and their children were Air and Day. Dark Night also gave birth to Death, Sleep, Dreams and the Fates and even the Hesperides and Eris. Then Mother Earth became the wide and stable base from which all life sprang. The Sky, which enveloped it with its immensity, was the greatest god at the beginning of the world.

THE TITANS

Mother Earth was the leading protagonist in cosmogony. It formed a union with Sky to make the first divine couple. From this union the Titans were born: The Oceanus, Tethys, Hyperion, Theia, Coeus, Phoebe, Creius, Iapetus, Cronus and Rhea.

Cronus and Rhea

Cronus, was the only son of Mother Earth to help her in taking revenge on his father Uranus (Sky). After castrating Uranus, Cronus took his place and cast out his brothers, the Hundred-Handed Ones and the Cyclopses. Then Cronus married his sister Rhea, but tried to ensure that none of their children would live, as his parents had told him that he would lose power to one of his own offspring. As soon as the children were born, Cronus devoured them: Hestia, Demeter, Hera, Pluto (Hades) and Poseidon, one after the other. As soon as Rhea realised she was pregnant again (with Zeus), she fled to Crete and bore the baby secretly. She left the baby to be brought up by the Oceanid Metis, giving Cronus a stone wrapped in swaddling-clothes which he took to be the newborn child and ate. So it happened that Zeus was saved.

Rhea delivers, to her husband and brother, the swaddled stone in place of Zeus. (AD 160, Museo Capitolino, Rome).

Zeus strikes the Titans, the brothers of Cronus,
with lightning in his attempt to confirm his supremacy and strengthen his power (Corfu, Achilleio).

THE BATTLE OF THE TITANS

As soon as Zeus grew up, he forced Cronus to swallow a potion which made him vomit up all the children he had swallowed. All the brothers and sisters then joined forces to liberate the Hundred-Handed Ones and the Cyclopses, and they declared war on Cronus, whose allies were his brothers, the Titans. All the gods young and old, took part in this war, the awe-inspiring Battle of the Titans, which resulted in Zeus' victory.

After the conclusion of the Battle of the Titans, Cronus and his brothers were bound in chains and flung into Tartarus, where the Hundred-Handed Ones stood guard over them.

Atlas

For some mythical figures the new order of things which now prevailed had painful consequences. Atlas, for example, one of the sons of the Titan Iapetus, was severely punished for his part in the war against Zeus. He was sent west to the ends of the earth, where lie the borders of Night, the child Chaos, and where the Hesperides guard their golden apples, as we shall see shortly. There he was doomed to stay, forever holding up the sky over the earth, or the earth and sky together, or the axis of the earth.

Bottom: Atlas offers the golden apples of the Hesperides to Heracles who had agreed to hold the sky on his shoulders. Behind Heracles, Athena helps him to support his burden by holding the sky with one hand. (Metope from the Temple of Zeus, Archaeological Museum of Olympia).

Right: Atlas supports the earth as a punishment for his participation against Zeus in the Titanomachia. (2nd century BC, National Museum of Naples).

THE BATTLE OF THE GIANTS

When Zeus punished the Titans, Mother Earth was angry that some of her children had been punished in this way (or, according to another version, because she did not think the gods were doing her enough honour). To take her revenge on him, she gave birth to the Giants.

The Giants were huge creatures with the hair of snakes and bodies whose lower parts were those of dragons. Their appearance inspired terror, and they were almost invincible. As soon as they were born they launched their attack on the gods of Olympus, hurling lighted torches, a rain of boulders and entire flaming trees. The mountains shook, and the air and sea were a hell of fire. The Olympian gods were thus forced to go to war once more, with Zeus and his thunderbolts in command, flanked by comrades capable of standing any test: Poseidon, Apollo, Hephaestus, the Fates, Dionysus and his retinue, and all the others. But the leading role in this battle was played by Athena, who was born during the course of the war, springing fully-armed from the head of Zeus. She immediately killed the Giant Pallas and took up her position by her father's side. The Battle of the Giants was prolonged, and would never have ended if Fate had not fulfilled itself as a mortal and fought side by side with the gods to bring them victory. This was Heracles, with whose help the Giants were killed off one by one.

Bottom: A scene depicting the Gigantomachia. On the left Athena grabs the Giant Alcyoneus by the hair.
On the right his mother, Gaia, begs for the life of her son. Nike flies towards Athena to crown her.
(180 BC, from the eastern frieze of the Pergamon Altar which was devoted to Zeus). Opposite: A Giant, naked but for a helmet,
wrestles with a lion. (525 BC, from the north frieze of the Treasury of the Siphnians at Delphi, Archaeological Museum of Delphi).

THE HUMAN RACE

O nce, in very early times when there were only immortal gods and no mortal beings in the world, it occurred to the immortals that they might create such beings to inhabit the earth. When this was done, Zeus ordered Prometheus and Epimetheus, sons of the Titan Iapetus, to endow the creatures of the earth with gifts and powers. Epimetheus asked of his brother that he should be allowed to share out the gifts of the gods. He bestowed beauty on one animal, strength on another, agility to counterbalance another's smallness of size, intelligence to offset yet another's bulk. And so Epimetheus went on giving out, decorating and sharing - yet he lacked the wisdom of his brother, for he gave all his gifts and weapons to the members of the animal kingdom and left man last, bare and defenceless, with no natural weapons.

Prometheus

P rometheus, the friend of man, stole wisdom from Athena and gave man reason, to square the balance. Then he stole fire from the forge of Hephaestus and gave it to man as a gift. Since then man has had fire to keep himself warm and alive, and to help him create. Prometheus became the protector of the human race, and taught it all he knew. But this angered Zeus, who did not want mankind to be helped to resemble the gods. And when he discovered that Prometheus had given man fire, he unleashed his thunder and lightning: until that time, fire had been reserved for the gods. Prometheus' punishment was a harsh one. Zeus chained him to a peak in the Caucasus, at the end of the world, where an eagle swooped down on him every day and pecked out his liver. But during the night Prometheus' liver grew back again, and so the next day he would undergo his torment once more. Thirty years were to pass before Heracles released Prometheus from his terrible ordeal.

Top: The torture of the Titans:
Atlas bears the sky with great effort whilst
Prometheus is tormented by an eagle tearing at his chest.
(550 BC, Laconian kylix, Vatican Museum, Rome).

Bottom:
Zeus punished
Prometheus severely for
his humanitarian attitude.
The father of the gods and man,
however, took care of his own son,
Heracles, who would release Prometheus
from his terrible toment 30 years later by killing
the eagle with an arrow and breaking his bonds.

Pandora

Hephaestus the smith, the god of fire, made the first woman in his forge. To begin with, she was a metal statue, but she was so beautiful that Zeus decided to give her life. All the other gods bestowed gifts upon her: beauty, grace, intelligence, skill and persuasiveness. But Hermes also gave her cunning and falsehood and Hera gave her the curiosity which would never let her rest.

Zeus sent Pandora to Epimetheus as a gift. He was so delighted by her beauty that he took her as his wife. As a wedding present, they were given a handsome box decorated with precious stones and gold. The box was locked, but Zeus gave the couple the key - saying to Pandora that if she wished to live happily with her husband, she should never open the box.

For a while, Epimetheus and Pandora lived quietly and happily together. But the curiosity which Hera had made part of Pandora's character proved to be more powerful in the end, and one day she opened the box. Out flew the miseries and misfortunes which have afflicted man since: disease, despair, pain and the other evils. But last of all came hope, like a little bird bearing a message of consolation for mankind.

Deucalion and Pyrrha

The time came when man turned evil, and there was nothing right or beautiful in what he did. Zeus decided to punish the human race by drowning it in a flood. The water that fell annihilated entire cities. But in order to ensure it would survive, he chose Deucalion and Pyrrha, who were the only good people. They survived in an ark and made sucrificies to the gods in gratitude.

After covering their faces, as Zeus had suggested they began to walk forward, dropping stones behind them but not looking round. Men sprang up from the stones which Deucalion dropped, and women from those left by Pyrrha. The couple also had children of their own, who were regarded as the offspring of Zeus. Of these, Hellen, their first-born, was regarded as the forefather of the Hellenes (Greeks).

The birth of Pandora.
(440 BC, volute krater, Oxford).

Deucalion and Pyrrha are depicted on the left next to the blacksmith Cyclopes on a sarcophagus of the 3rd century AD.

Chapter 2

The Gods

*T*he ancient divinities we have referred to at a certain point no longer satisfied the imagination or the yearnings of religion. People then wanted more actively involved gods to keep them company in their daily lives and to take a position in regard to their problems. Thus, the victors of Olympus grew large in their imagination and came to rule over religious worship. So powerful and at the same time so vulnerable to human weaknesses, they regulated the fortunes and the lives of those they both loved and hated.

These gods shared all of mankind's virtues and faults. They were vengeful but also excessively generous, while at the same time being propitiated by the material sacrifices they were offered by the faithful. There was no job or social need that was not connected to the worship of some god: from farming to education, from the fine arts to hunting, from military valour to love. Here one finds certain gods more carefree and fun-loving, who gave life its necessary zest with their high spirits and merriment; this facet is to be found in the religious worship of Dionysus, Pan and Aphrodite.

An endeavor will be made to present the gods that made up the Pantheon of Olympus and then to mention the lesser gods who are also of great interest.

Even more minor deities will be mentioned as Greek mythology personified all human concepts and emotions.

Thus, having become acquainted with the distinctive characteristics of each god, we will be better able to understand their presence and participation in the adventures of the heroes we will encounter below.

Representation of the chryselephantine statue of Zeus which, because of its grace and majesty, is considered to be one of the Seven Wonders of the Ancient World.

After gaining power over earth and heaven,
the twelve gods of Olympus shared out
responsibilities and posts amongst themselves
in accordance with the wishes of Zeus.
They lived on Mt. Olympus,
the highest mountain in Greece, but they often
came down and mingled with human beings,
to help them, to punish them, to regulate their
fortunes and even to unite with them and give
birth to children. The children born of gods
and mortals were called demi-gods, and they
possessed rare skills. They performed a whole host
of heroic feats and were admired by all.
The food of the gods was called ambrosia and
their drink nectar - a drink reserved for them
alone. But they willingly accepted the sacrifices
and offerings of men, with animals slaughtered
or burned to honour them or in the shape of the
other fruits of the earth. The gods kept their
promises, especially when made under oath.

Their most fearful oath was that sworn
"by the waters of the Styx".
The gods of Olympus were almost omnipotent,
in the sense that the power of each stopped
where the jurisdiction of another began, since
each had his or her own realm of power.
Only Zeus was truly omnipotent.
The gods resembled men in many ways.
The twelve gods occupied a special position
in the religious consciousness of the ancient
Greek world: "by the twelve gods of Olympus"
was a sacred oath which demonstrated
the respect the Greeks felt for these figures
who determined the fate of the world
and all those in it. Let us now get to
know them a little better.
The names of the twelve gods of Olympus
were: **Zeus, Hera, Athena, Poseidon, Demeter,
Apollo, Artemis, Hermes, Ares, Aphrodite,
Hephaestus** and **Hestia**.

ZEUS, *the lord of heaven and earth,*
the father of gods and humans

Zeus, the most powerful of the immortal Olympian gods, was born in the Diktaean cave and hidden by his mother Rhea in the Idaean cave on Crete, where he grew up on the milk provided by the goat Amaltheia and in the care of the Nymphs.

His weapon was the thunderbolt, and his domain included both the earth and the sky. The lawful and perpetual wife of Zeus was Hera, who was always his steady, faithful companion in his life and work.

Together they had Ares, Hebe, Eileithia and Hephaestus. Zeus had countless love affairs with other goddesses and mortal women, often arousing the jealousy of Hera. In those relationships Zeus sired many other children, some of whom were gods, and others demi-gods and heroes. Zeus loved and protected all his children, who often attracted the rage of Hera. Zeus was the god who maintained the balance of justice. His role was not only to punish and avenge, but also to share in the pain of the unfortunate and help to relieve their sufferings by dispensing justice. The charismatic leaders of antiquity were described as "born of Zeus" or "nurtured by Zeus" when the speaker wished to praise the prudence of their government or their sense of justice.

With divine majesty, Zeus raises his fearsome weapon, the thunderbolt. (470 BC, bronze statue from Dodona, National Archaeological Museum of Athens).

*Zeus, charmed by his beauty,
leads Ganymede to Olympus.
(480 BC, terracotta group,
Archaeological Museum of Olympia).*

Zeus and Europa

T he beautiful Europa, the daughter of Agenora and Telephassa, was among the young women Zeus fell in love with. The maiden was playing with her girl friends on the shore at Sidon and her charms made the father of gods and men fall in love with her. In order to get near her he transformed himself into a pure white bull and went and lay at her feet.

As Europa took courage, she began to sport with the bull. But as soon as she sat on his back he leapt up and plunged into the sea. She cried for help in vain. The bull swam further and further from the shore.

Europa took firm hold of his horns to keep from falling off and in that way they reached Crete. At the spring of Gortys the couple made love under the shadow of the plane trees. Since that time the trees have never shed their leaves, because they covered the love of a god. Zeus and Europa had three sons: the legendary Minos, the brave Sarpedon and the just Radamanthys.

The abduction of Europa. Third century mosaic from the 'House of Europa' (Kos).

HERA, *the patron goddess of the family and married women*

H era, the worthy spouse of Zeus, was the patron of marriage and married women. Her own relationship with Zeus long predated their marriage, and they used to meet in secret from their parents. But after the twelve gods took power and Zeus began to reign on Olympus, they were able to get married. Hera intervenes in many of the myths, and brought up numerous children apart from her own. She punished infidelity and took fierce revenge on her husband's paramours.

Head of Hera. (420 BC, National Archaeological Museum of Athens).

Zeus and Hera. The two gods hold the royal sceptres and converse. Zeus, crowned, also holds a kylix. (Circa 430 BC, kylix, British Museum, London).

ATHENA, *the goddess of wisdom*

After the victory of the Olympian gods in the Battle of the Titans, Zeus formed a union with Metis, daughter of Oceanus and Tithys. Her parents told Zeus that the fruit of the union would first be Athena, whose bravery and wisdom would rival those of her father, and later a son, who would be more clever than Zeus and might, one day, be a menace to his throne. Zeus responded by swallowing Metis. But the time for Athena to be born was drawing near, and so Zeus ordered Prometheus (or Hephaestus in some versions) to lay open his head with an axe. All were amazed to see Athena spring fully-armed from Zeus' head, brandishing her spear.

The young goddess stood side by side with her father during the Battle of the Giants, where she managed to overcome Enceladus, casting him down and throwing the whole of Sicily on top of him to immobilise him. Although she was the goddess of war, she was not warlike. Clever and wise, she helped heroes such as Perseus, Achilles and Odysseus - though her love for these figures had nothing erotic about it. Athena and Artemis had decided never to marry - even other gods - and to keep their virginity.

According to the traditional account, Poseidon and Athena quarrelled over which of them should be the patron of the city of Athens and whose name the city would bear. In the end, it was decided that each of them should make the city a gift, and the donor of the gift which the other gods judged most valuable would become the patron of the city.

Poseidon struck the rock of the Acropolis with his trident, and water gushed forth. Athena stamped her foot on the ground, and the world's first olive tree sprang up. The olive tree was thus sacred, and even in very early times was regarded as a symbol of peace. Since the time gods gave the victory to Athena, the city of Athens has borne her name and has enjoyed her protection.

'Varvakeion Athena',
a Roman copy of Pheidias'
chryselephantine goddess which
was in the Parthenon.

Relief depiction of the goddess Athena
known as 'The Mourning Athena'.
The goddess is barefoot but wears a Doric
peplos with a belt at the waist and a helmet.
(460 BC, relief, Acropolis Museum of Athens).

The majestic 'Poseidon
of Artemision'
(460 BC, bronze statue,
National Archaeological
Museum of Athens).

POSEIDON, *god of the sea*

P oseidon, god of the sea, was one of the deities whom the Greeks most revered: he, Zeus and Hera were the Olympian gods always depicted as eldest. In his gold chariot, Poseidon drives back and forth across his realm of oceans and seas among the waves which do not even wet him, surrounded by a company of happy dolphins. Poseidon's amatory exploits involved many of the goddesses and a respectable number of mortal females, on whom he bestowed numerous children. Among them (with their mothers in brackets) were: Triton (Amphitrite), Polyphemus (Thoosa), Antaeus (Mother Earth), and numerous others. Since he embraced the world and influenced it, he was often known by the titles of "Girder of the World", "World Shaker", "Ocean-Claimer", "God of Oceans", "Emperor of the Sea", and many others.

Floor mosaic depicting Poseidon defeating the Giant Polybotes.

APOLLO, *or Phoebus,*
the god of light, music and prophecy

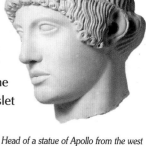

Head of a statue of Apollo from the west pediment of the Temple of Zeus at Olympia. (457 BC, Archaeological Museum of Olympia).

A s the children of Zeus and Leto, Apollo and his sister belonged to the second generation of Olympian gods. Pursued by Hera, the pregnant Leto searched desperately for somewhere to give birth to her children. In fear of the queen of the gods, all the Greek cities drove her away. In the end, the barren islet of Delos - then called Ortygia - gave her sanctuary, and it was there that Apollo and Artemis were born. As soon as the god of the sun, of prophecy and of music saw the light of day, the island began to glow and the whole world shone.

As Apollo grew, he performed astounding feats, including ridding Delphi of the dragon Pytho, whom he killed with his arrows. As a result, he was called Pythian Apollo, the Pythian Games took their name and the priestess of the oracle became known as the Pythia. The Pythia squatted on the sacred tripod of Apollo inside the god's oracle, and made prophecies.

Apollo was a handsome god: tall and well-built, he had flowing locks and enjoyed frequent romantic encounters with nymphs and mortal maidens.

Apart from his achievements in music, the pastroral arts and prophecy, Apollo was also a god of war, with particular skill in shooting arrows over great distances. Mankind paid him the highest honours, dedicating to him sanctuaries, oracles, athletic contests and sacrifices.

Mosaic depicting Apollo hunting Daphne, daughter of the Peneus river.
In the picture Daphne has reached her father and is transforming into a laurel tree.

The god Apollo, crowned and holding
his lyre, during a libation.
(490 BC, interior of a kylix,
Archaeological Museum of Delphi).

ARTEMIS, *goddess of the moon and the hunt*

A rtemis, the daughter of Zeus, was born to Leto on the same day as her brother Apollo. She was the goddess of the hunt, and of the moon. When she was a girl, she begged Zeus to allow her to remain unmarried and so she roamed the forests, girt with her bow and arrow and accompanied by deer and her beloved wild beasts. Artemis took part in the Battle of the Giants, where with the help of Heracles she killed the Giant Gration.

She was a vengeful deity, punishing all those who showed her disrespect. She protected hunters and the innocent. One well-known story is that of the revenge that she and Apollo took on Niobe, daughter of Tantalus. Niobe boasted that she had given birth to fourteen children, while Leto had only two. The two gods avenged this slight on their mother by shooting Niobe's children dead with, their arrows, Apollo the boys and Artemis the girls.

Artemis on a relief from the gathering of the gods on the east frieze of the Parthenon. (447 - 432 BC, Acropolis Museum of Athens).

The goddess Artemis. (Second half of the 2nd century AD, Museum of Kos).

DEMETER, *the goddess of agriculture*

D emeter was the goddess of fertility, a mother-deity associated with the earth who protected cultivated soil, wheat in particular. She was also the goddess of the birth of the world: all the flowers, fruits and other living things were the gifts of Demeter. Demeter is closely linked with her daughter Persephone, whose father was Zeus, and the two female deities are usually mentioned together.

The abduction of Persephone

Persephone, Demeter's only daughter, grew up to be a happy child in the company of her mother and the other goddesses, until one day Pluto fell in love with her and abducted her. Persephone was picking lilies in a field, when suddenly the earth opened beneath her feet and Pluto carried her off to the underworld. When Demeter discovered that her daughter was missing, she began to search for her. She wandered anxiously and sadly, day and night, across the entire known world. While she was absent in Eleusis, the earth was barren, the crops withered, no plant blossomed or bore fruit and mankind suffered from starvation. It was then that Zeus ordered Pluto to send Persephone home, since Demeter was threatening to prevent the earth from bearing even a single stalk of wheat. Pluto agreed to send his wife back to her mother in the upper world - but before doing so, he cunningly made her eat a pomegranate seed, which was enough to bind her to the underworld for ever. And so a contract had to be made with Pluto: for eight months of the year Persephone would live in the upper world, with her mother, and for four she would stay in Hades, with her husband. Demeter agreed to this, and before long the fields were full of wheat, the trees were in leaf, the earth was carpeted with flowers and all the plants were heavy with fruit. Since then, everything has been green and fertile for eight months of the year. But for the four months when Demeter loses her daughter, it is as if nature has died.

Left: The god of Hades throws seeds on the field which Demeter has already ploughed. According to one belief, the god of the underworld had to accept the seed for the crop to be good. (430 - 420 BC, red-figure pelike, National Archaeological Museum of Athens).

Right: Terracotta votive offering tablet with representations of the Eleusinian Mysteries. (4th century BC, National Archaeological Museum of Athens).

The famous Italian painter S. Botticelli's work 'The Birth of Aphrodite' was inspired by Greek mythology. (Florence, 1480).

APHRODITE
the goddess of beauty and love

There are two different myths about the birth of Aphrodite, goddess of love and beauty. One we have already mentioned: that she was the daughter of Zeus and Dione. The other relates that she sprang from the seed of Uranus when his genitals fell into the sea after his mutilation by Cronus.

Aphrodite was the patron of love and lovers, and her favourite pastime was causing the gods to fall in love with mortal women. She enjoyed weaving plots and enmeshing the gods in love affairs - especially Zeus, whom we find embroiled in various intrigues at different times. Nor was Aphrodite herself to be left out of the game. Although married to the lame god Hephaestus, she embarked on an affair with Ares.

Homer tell us all about this scandalous tale in The Iliad.

Her union with Ares brought Aphrodite the four children we have already mentioned: Eros, Deimus, Phobus and Harmony. Aphrodite was particularly fond of roses and myrtle, and her chariot was drawn by two doves, her favourite bird.

Marble head of Aphrodite, the work of a Greek sculptor working on Cyprus. (Beginning of the 4th century BC, from the gymnasium of Salamis).

The Venus de Milo. (2nd century BC, the Louvre, Paris).

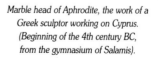

Right: The god Pan attempts to embrace the naked Aphrodite who wards him off with her sandal. Eros is between them, smiling. (100 BC, National Archaeological Museum of Athens).

HERMES,

the god of commerce and prophecy,
the messenger of the gods,
and bearer of dead souls

H ermes was the son of Zeus and Maia, a beautiful girl who was one of the Pleiads. Even as a baby it was clear that he was going to be crafty beyond compare and a sly god. While still in swaddling-clothes, he stole the oxen of his half-brother Apollo and hid them so well that Apollo needed all his oracular talents and techniques to find them. In fact, he might never have found them at all without the help of Zeus, fair-minded as ever. The incident passed without rancour and the half-brothers were reconciled when Hermes presented Apollo with a lyre he had himself invented and made out of the shell of a tortoise. Apollo, in return, made him a gift of the oxen and taught him divination. Hermes was the god of commerce and theft, and he served as the herald of the gods. There were wings on his helmet and his heels, and he bore a sceptre. Apart from his task of taking messages wherever Zeus sent him, he was also entrusted with the task of escorting the souls of those who died to Hades.

White lekythos on which are depicted a female
figure (not visible here), Charon and Hermes.
The very important painter who made
it was living in the time of Pheidias
and is known as 'the Artist of Sabouroff'.
(The National Museum).

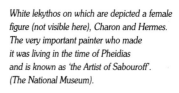

Hermes and the newborn Dionysus,
the famous statue by Praxiteles.
(330 BC, Archaeological Museum of Olympia).

ARES, *the god of War*

Ares, the fierce god of war, is always shown in armour and wearing a helmet, ready for battle. Wherever war and bloodshed broke out, wherever there was combat, Ares was to be found. As a result, he was rarely worshipped and we know of no cities he was patron of. The son of Zeus and Hera, he often fought with the other gods - even with his own father. He was worshipped at Thebes, where he was believed to be the forefather of the royal dynasty, since Harmony, wife of king Cadmus of Thebes, was his daughter by Aphrodite. Ares was the father of other children, too: Cycnus, Diomedes of Thrace (the owner of man-eating horses), Lycaon, Meleager, Dryas and Oenomaos.

Castor, Ares and Pollux (or according to others Poseidon, Ares and Hermes) repel four Giants from above.
(400 - 300 BC, red-figure pelike, National Archaeological Museum of Athens).

HEPHAESTUS, *the god of fire and art*

Hephaestus, son of Zeus and Hera, was the god of fire, metal-working and art. He made jewellery and other works of art, but was also prepared to turn out everything from sceptres to thrones, amphorae to golden robots. It was he who, at the request of Thetis, made Achilles' armour and beat out the superb scene depicted on the shield.

Hephaestus' workshop was on Lemnos, but all places where there were volcanoes and fire belonged to him. He was strong of arm, like any other blacksmith who spends all day with hammer and anvil, but his legs were weak. In addition, Hephaestus was lame, a fact for which there were two explanations: according to one, Zeus was quarrelling with Hera one day when the young Hephaestus dared to intervene on his mother's side. In his rage, Zeus picked Hephaestus up by the leg and hurled him from Olympus. He fell to earth on Lemnos, where the Sintians, a Thracian people who had emigrated to the island, took care of him - but he was left with a lame leg. The other tale says that he was born lame, and that it was Hera, in shame, who decided to throw him off Olympus. He fell into the Ocean, where Tethys and Eurynome saved him and brought him up in a sea cave. Although Hephaestus was extremely ugly, we always find him in the company of beautiful women, including Chare (beauty personified) and Aglaea, the youngest of the three Graces.

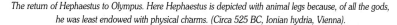

The return of Hephaestus to Olympus. Here Hephaestus is depicted with animal legs because, of all the gods, he was least endowed with physical charms. (Circa 525 BC, Ionian hydria, Vienna).

HESTIA, *the goddess of family peace*

As her name ("hearth") indicates, Hestia was the personification of the family home. The eldest daughter of Cronus and Rhea, Hestia asked her brother Zeus to let her remain a virgin, despite the fact that both Poseidon and Apollo wanted her for a wife. The serenity of Hestia's life on Olympus and the stability of her position there meant that she played little part in events and her presence is confined largely to the world of ideas.

In this representation, Hestia, the goddess of family peace, is shown holding a branch with fruits while Ganymede, protected by Zeus who holds the lightning bolt, fills his guardian's glass with wine.

THE LESSER GODS

Besides the twelve Olympian gods there were other gods who were also frequently worshipped, the difference being their seat was not on Olympus or they were the child of a god and a mortal, such as Asclepius. The worship of these gods is of great interest because it is often identified with the way of life, the religious ceremonies and the civilization of a given period.

The god Dionysus from a table mosaic from Paphos.
The god of wine sits on a stool and proffers a bunch of grapes (Paphos, House of Dionysus).

Dionysus, *god of wine and gaiety*

S emele was one of the daughters of Cadmus, king of Thebes. Zeus fell in love with her beauty, but their relationship did not escape the notice of the jealous Hera. In order to harm Semele, Hera told her that if she wished to be regarded as Zeus' wife she would have to see him in all his glory, as he had been on the day of his wedding to Hera. Although Zeus tried to dissuade her, Semele fell for Hera's deception and insisted on having this proof of love. But when Zeus gave in and appeared in her chambers mounted on his chariot amidst thunder and lightning, casting his bolts of fire, he set the palace alight and Semele died from a bolt of lightning - or perhaps he just scared her to death.

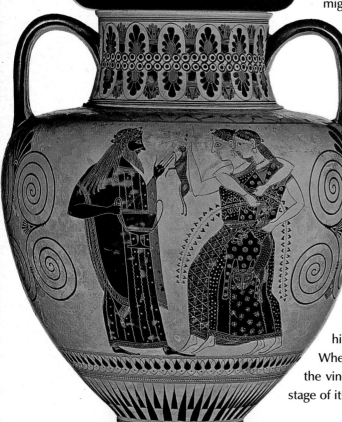

However, she had been carrying Dionysus in her womb for six months. So that the baby might not burn to death, Mother Earth quickly caused cool ivy to grow and protect him from the flames. Zeus picked up the baby - still in an embryonic state - made an opening in his thigh, and left Dionysus there until it was time for him to be born, so as to spare him the jealousy of Hera. When the day came, Zeus broke the stitches and brought his son Dionysus out into the light. As a result of these adventures, Dionysus was described as "fire-born", "thigh- sewn" and "twice-born".

But the rage of Hera haunted him - to the point where it drove him mad and he wandered aimlessly. Rhea cured him, and he continued on his travels. Wherever he went, he spread the culture of the vine and the rituals associated with every stage of its cultivation.

Dionysus and the Maenads.

Right: Bronze krater depicting Dionysus and Ariadne in a tender scene. (350 - 330 BC, Archaeological Museum of Thessaloniki).

Dionysus is the god of wine, of green growing things, and of the fertility of the vineyard. The Dionysian cult was associated with wine, dance and everything that gets mankind out of its daily rut. The Dionysian "orgies" were organised festivals with religious rites and included holy works: the word "orgy", which is Greek, originally meant "mystery". The rituals were accompanied by the chanting of the dithyramb, the song in worship of Dionysus. The company of Dionysus was made up of Nymphs, Sileni, Satyrs and Maenads. The Sileni were

men with the legs and tails of horses, who pursued the Nymphs and revelled with them in caves. The Maenads, or Bacchae, were women who personified the orgiastic spirits of nature.

The triumph of Dionysus.
A procession showing the triumphant
return of the god from India
on a chariot pulled by panthers.
These mosaic depicitions are from
the 'House of Dionysus' in Paphos (Cyprus).

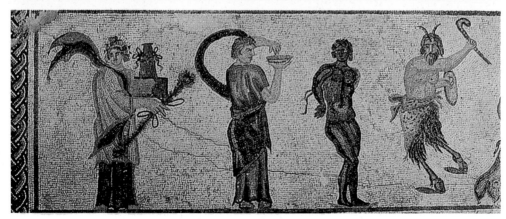

Asclepius, *the god of medicine*

A sclepius was a hero, and also the god of medicine. The son of Apollo by Coronis (or Arsinoe, according to others), Asclepius spent time in youth with the Centaur Chiron, as did almost all of the important men of his time. The wise Centaur taught him medicine, at which Asclepius became most proficient. Asclepius' wife was Epione, and the myths give him two sons, Podaleirius and Machaon, both of them physicians, and five daughters, Aceso, Iaso, Panacea, Aegle and Hygeia. After his death Zeus set Asclepius among the stars holding a curative serpent.

Statue of Asclepius from the Roman period.
(Museum of Rhodes).

Mosaic depicting the arrival of Asclepius on Kos (2nd - 3rd centuries AD).

Hygeia, the most important daughter of Asclepius, was the personification of psychic and bodily health. There is no specific myth related to her. She belonged to the assembly of Asclepius and was worshipped together with him. Asclepius' art of medicine was continued by his descendants, the Asclepiads, the most famous of whom was Hippocrates.

Iris,
the messenger of the gods

Iris was descended from the line of Oceanus, and Thaumas and Electra were her parents. She is the personification of the rainbow, a symbol of union between the sky and the earth (Uranus and Mother Earth). Iris is depicted with wings, dressed in a gauzy veil, and she serves Zeus as a messenger much as Hermes does, passing on the news and the orders of the gods.

Statue of the goddess Hygeia with the snake. At the feet of the goddess is a small Eros. The statue is in the building with the mosaics of Europa. (2nd century AD, Museum of Kos).

Helios, *the god of light*

A depiction of the god Helios. The god was also depicted in the famous statue the 'Colossus of Rhodes', one of the Seven Wonders of the Ancient World.

Helios, the sun god, was older than the gods of Olympus. The son of the Titan Hyperion and the Titaness Theia, he was descended from Uranus and Mother Earth. Io (the dawn) and Oceanus were his brother and sister, and he had a number of famous children: the sorceress Circe, Aeetes the king of Colchis, Pasiphae the wife of Minos, and Perses.

Helios is shown as a handsome man whose golden locks are crowned with the gold rays of the sun. He is depicted driving across the sky in his fiery chariot, drawn by horses of unsurpassed speed. The sun god is above the Earth and the Ocean, in his chariot all day, using a craft like a huge, deep cup to cross the sea. Helios sees everything, and in various myths is a witness to acts of good and evil.

Hades or Pluto,
the god of the underworld

Hades, the brother of Zeus, Poseidon and Hera, was the god who ruled the underworld, and he came third in the hierarchy when Creation was shared out amongst Zeus, Poseidon and himself.

In his kingdom of darkness, Hades was harsh and ruthless. None of the inhabitants of the underworld was permitted to return to the land of the living. He had various demons and servants, such as Charon, who as ferryman took souls across the river Acheron in his boat, to the kingdom of the dead on the other side. His fee was one obol - a coin which was buried with each dead person.

Pluto leading Persephone to his dark kingdom. Hecate lights the way in front and Hermes accompanies them. (360 - 350 BC, Apulian krater, British Museum, London).

Priapus, *a fertility god*

Priapus looked rather like Pan. The sources call him the son of Dionysus by the Nymph Chione, or of Dionysus and Aphrodite, or Hermes, or even of Zeus. He grew up in Lampsacus, which he was reputed to have founded. Priapus was the god of fertility - in the plant world as well as the animal kingdom - and of physical love. The excessively large penis of Priapus, was a projection and representation of the male organ as the bringer of life and creation.

Pan, *the god of forests and bucolic life*

Pan, an elemental figure in Greek nature, was the god of shepherds and herds. Even in earliest times, he is depicted as a kind of demon, halfman, half-goat, with a weather-beaten face, a pointed chin, a beard, horns on his forehead and a hairy body. Agile in his moments and cheerful, Pan embodied the bucolic life lived by cool springs and in shady woods. He was a highly sexual fellow and engaged in erotic games with Nymphs or young boys. Pan spent his time grazing his flocks and playing his pan-pipes, an instrument which he - as we can see from the name - is supposed to have invented.

Pan's background is far from clear. He was born in Arcadia, and may have been the son of Cronus (with Rhea) or Hermes. According to one myth, when the Nymph who was his mother gave birth to him and saw what a monster she had brought into the world, she abandoned him. But Hermes found him, wrapped him in the skin of a hare and took him to Olympus. The gods found him appealing, and allowed him to stay with them. He was a particular favourite of Dionysus, who took him travelling.

The god Pan sitting on a rock.
A statuette from the Hellenistic period.
(National Archaeological Museum of Athens).

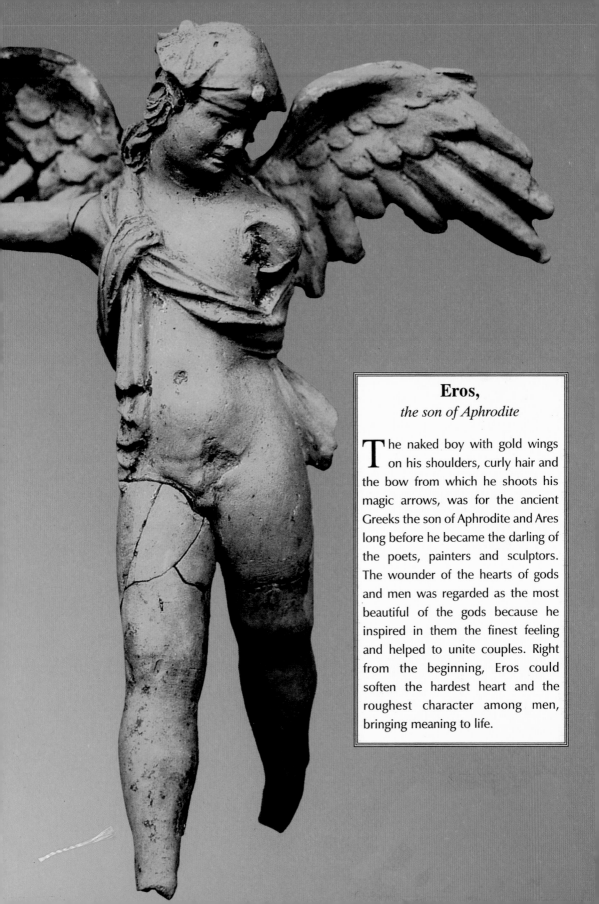

Eros,
the son of Aphrodite

The naked boy with gold wings on his shoulders, curly hair and the bow from which he shoots his magic arrows, was for the ancient Greeks the son of Aphrodite and Ares long before he became the darling of the poets, painters and sculptors. The wounder of the hearts of gods and men was regarded as the most beautiful of the gods because he inspired in them the finest feeling and helped to unite couples. Right from the beginning, Eros could soften the hardest heart and the roughest character among men, bringing meaning to life.

Themis, *the goddess of justice*

Themis, the goddess of justice, looked after moral order among gods and men. She protected the weak and ill-treated. Themis possessed the gift of divination, and had her own oracle at Delphi before it was taken over by Apollo, to whom she passed on her oracular skills. Themis was the daughter of Uranus and Mother Earth, and the sister of Cronus, Rhea, Mnemosyne, Oceanus and the other Titans.

Her union with Zeus produced the Horae ("hours"), Eunomia ("order of law"), Dice ("justice") and Eirene ("Peace"), who looked after the works of men, along with the three Fates. The first of the three Fates, Clotho, spun the thread of human life; the second, Lachese, shared out joy and sorrow, and the third, Atropos, cut the thread to bring life to an end.

The Erinnyes

When Cronus mutilated the Sky, castrating him with a sickle, the blood that dripped to Earth gave birth to the Erinnyes (the Furies): Ellecto, Tisiphone and Megaera. Cruel, implacable goddesses, they exercised control over conscience and persecuted every transgression. Sometimes they inflicted punishment in the personification of remorse after an unjust act and sometimes like terrible figures with a death-like mien, they hunted down and punished all hideous crimes and incest.

The Erinnyes were a form of "divine justice" who above and beyond the justice meted out by Zeus, punished all those who transgressed the rules of ethics.

Marble statue of the goddess Themis from Rhamnous (3rd century BC, National Archaeol. Museum of Athens).

Sea Divinities

The sea had its own ruling spirits which belonged to the Kingdom of Poseidon.

Nireas,
the eldest son of Pondus and Earth and the father of the Nereids, was an elderly mariner with a sweet visage who could change shape.

Proteus
was the patron of sea creatures.

Triton,
the son of Poseidon and Amphitrite, was half man and half fish and his sisters were the Nereids.

Glaucus,
a sea god who was originally a man, was later transformed into a sea spirit. His form was human while his torso was covered with shells and seaweed.

OTHER LESSER GODS

B esides the important Gods already mentioned, there are other lesser ones. These gods are by and large the personifications of abstract concepts.

Eris

Eris, the goddess of discord. She was the daughter of Night and the sister and companion of Ares. This disputatious goddess was present at every quarrel or disagreement.

Hebe

Hebe. Her name means youth and is the joy and the beauty this age gives to human beings. Daughter of Zeus and Hera, she offered nectar to the gods. Heracles married her when he was received on Olympus.

Peitho (Conviction)

Peitho ("conviction"). Daughter of Oceanus, friend and assistant of Aphrodite, she convinced young girls to overcome their hesitations and give themselves over to love.

Tyche (Fortune)

This was a goddess without any mythological content, being the personification of the abstract concept of luck.

Ate

Ate, which means misfortune, was the personification of infatuation.

Litai

The Litai were the daughters of Zeus who fixed up whatever evil Ate did.

Hubris

Hubris was the personification of arrogance.

Nemesis

Nemesis was the goddess who brought rest to gods and people, granting them forgetfulness and relaxation.

Thanatos (Death)

Thanatos ("death"), the brother of Sleep, was a figure that was confused with Hadas, Charon, and Hermes the bearer of dead souls. Sisyphus was the only one who managed to outwit death.

Anagi (Need)

Anagi ("need") was the personfication of the forces which made the decisions of Fate imperative

Iacchus

Iacchus was the god who directed the ceremony of initiation into the Eleusinian Mysteries. His name is derived from the cry of the faithful there, ("Iacche"), during the ceremony. Others consider him related to Dionysus (Bacchus) while still others believe he was the son of the goddess Demeter.

Chapter 3

The Heroes

During those ancient times mankind went through some difficult moments. The dangers of that far-off period were manfold: invincible monsters, terrible villains who ravaged a region and made it uninhabitable, horrible diseases and hideous creatures with human characteristics who were immortal by their divine nature. Then the gods sent to earth their heroes, most of whom were demi-gods.

Demi-gods were those born of a god and a mortal mother. Some were destined to become known on a panhellenic scale and others remained local heroes. The heroes were protected by the gods; they were magnificent beings and endowed with many advantages: power, virility, intelligence, magnanimity and ingenuity. Sometimes they appear as enlightened leaders who leave their throne to guide a war with a holy purpose to victory, such as Odysseus, and other times they are brave and robust young men such as Heracles, fighting to make sure that good prevails.

They take on dangerous missions to fulfill a moral obligation, for the heart of a pretty princess, the acquisition of a kingdom or even the fulfillment of a divine wish. These heroes usually had a god to protect and assist them in the realization of their difficult task. Frequently, this god rescued them from danger and punished those who were plotting against them. Quite often the gods clashed with one another because of the heroes they had under their protection.

The heroes led a very turbulent life. One could say they were predestined in this by fate and enlisted in the struggle for good. They were glorified for their feats and acquired fame, and several of them even gained immortality.

HERACLES

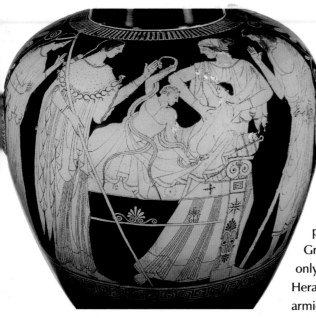

Heracles, as a baby,
strangles the snakes which Hera had sent to kill him.
(Circa 480 BC, red-figure stamnos, the Louvre, Paris).

Heracles in youth

As an adolescent, Heracles was strong, vigorous, disobedient and unusually well-developed. At eighteen, he had already accomplished his first feat, killing the lion of Cithairon which was ravaging the flocks on the mountain and which no one had been able to dispose of. At about the same time, this tall, handsome adolescent was out walking one day when he came to a fork in the road.

One branch was a fine, broad path to start with, but in the distance it could be seen to narrow. At the start of this road stood a beautiful woman in gaudy clothes. The other road was initially narrow and beset with thorns, but further along it broadened and was strewn with flowers. Here there was a woman of gentle and modest appearance, dressed simply but with nobility.

- "Who are you?", Heracles asked the women.

- "Come to me", said the first woman. "I will make you happy. My name is Sin".

- "No, follow me", said the second. "You will gain the gratitude, respect and affection of all. My name is Virtue".

The name of Heracles is identified with power, heroism and majesty. This demi-god, who became a symbol as his fame reached every corner of the then known world, represents a true superman!

There was no "labour" that was beyond the power of Heracles. The problems which appeared in nearly all Greek societies, as well as outside it, could only be solved by one man and that was Heracles. He did battle with villains, monsters, armies, gods, natural forces, illness and even with death!

Heracles was a demi-god, endowed with supernatural gifts but also with human weaknesses. He belonged to the Perseid family and was born at Thebes, supposedly to a mortal father, Amphitryon, and Alcemene. However, his real father was Zeus, who took advantage of Amphitryon's absence one night to disguise himself as the mortal man and sleep with Alcemene.

And so Heracles came to be born, with his twin brother Iphicles: he is held by the myth to be the true son of Amphitryon, since he was conceived the following evening, on his father's return.

The goddess Hera was not long in manifesting her jealousy of the infant, who was able to demonstrate his divine origins at the age of only eight months.

One evening, when Alcemene had put the twins to bed, Hera sent two enormous snakes to squeeze them to death in their cradle. Iphicles began to cry, but Heracles showed no fear and seized one snake in each hand, killing them.

The Nemean Lion.

The Stymphalian Birds.

The Oxen of Geryon.

Cerberus.

The Golden Apples of the Hesperides.

The demi-god
Heracles

*In the years that followed, Heracles' fame
began to spread and no one could rival him
in strength or bravery. Creon, king of Thebes,
wed Heracles to his daughter Megara,
to honour him for his bravery.
But Hera was still on the lookout to harm him,
and she sent madness to overcome him.
In a fit of insanity, Heracles slew the children
he had had with Megara. When he recovered
and realised what he had done,
his first thought was suicide, but in the end he decided
to seek the advice of the Delphic oracle.
Pythia told him that to expiate the death of his
children he would have to go to Argos
and put himself in the service of his cousin,
king Eurystheus, for twelve years.
On Eurystheus' instructions, Heracles was to embark
on the series of labours which would grant him
immortality and gain him access to Olympus.
And so the popular hero presented himself before
the king of Argos who, out of personal malice
towards Heracles, made him risk his life
in the most incredibly dangerous encounters with
all the most fearsome monsters and supernatural
beings he could imagine.*

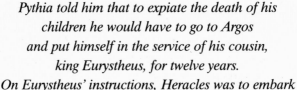

The Augean Stables.

The Girdle of Queen Hippolyta.

The Ceryneian Hind.

The Erymanthian Boar.

The Horses of Diomedes.

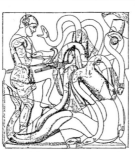

The Lernaean Hydra.

The Cretan Bull.

THE TWELVE LABOURS OF HERACLES

Heracles wrestling with the Nemean Lion. (Circa 510 BC, detail from a black-figure amphora, Brescia).

The Lion of Nemea

The first labour of Heracles was a superhuman achievement, because apart from being of supernatural size and ferocity in devouring herds and human beings, the Lion of Nemea had its lair in an inaccessible cave with two entrances. Heracles attempted to hunt the Lion down with his bow and arrow, but in vain. Then he decided to wall up one entrance to the cave and use his club to drive it inside. Once inside the cave, Heracles seized the Lion, wrestled with it and, with his superhuman strength, eventually strangled it. Heracles skinned the Lion and wore its hide, the head of which served as a kind of helmet. It is in this lion-skin that Heracles is depicted in many paintings. As soon as Eurystheus caught sight of him wearing it, he hastened to hide, in awe of the hero's spectacular feat.

The Lernaean Hydra

Heracles attacking the Lernaean Hydra with an axe. (Beginning of the 5th century BC, black-figure amphora, the Louvre, Paris).

The Hydra of Lernaea had been wreaking havoc among the crops and flocks of the area. Even the breath emitted by its snake's heads was so poisonous that it could kill anyone standing nearby. Heracles fired burning arrows at the monster to drive it out of its lair, and as soon as it appeared he began to cat off its heads with an axe. His efforts were in vain, however, since it sprouted two heads for every one that Heracles could cut off.

Heracles was forced to kill the crab first, after which he called for the help of his nephew, Iolaos of Thebes. Iolaos set fire to a nearby forest, and as Heracles smote the heads of the Hydra he cauterised the necks with a fiery torch so as to prevent the appearance of fresh heads. After cutting off the central head - which had been presumed to be immortal - Heracles buried it and turned it into a huge rock. The blood of the Lernaean Hydra contained a very powerful poison, and the tip of any arrow dipped in it became fatal.

The Hind of Ceryneia

The next labour which Eurystheus set for Heracles was to catch the hind with the golden horns which lived at Oenoe and bring it alive to Mycenae. The hind, which lived on the Arcadian mountain of Ceryneia, hid even from Artemis herself and it grazed throughout Arcadia and in the mountains sacred to the goddess above Argos. Heracles hunted it for a whole year without ever getting close enough to loose an arrow. In the end, Heracles managed to trap the animal, but on the way back he fell in with Apollo and Artemis, who were angered by his act. Heracles apologised to the goddess and she forgave him once he had taken the beast alive to Mycenae.

The Boar of Erymanthus

The Boar, whose capture was Eurystheus' fourth labour, was a fearsome wild beast which lived on Erymanthus, in southwest Arcadia. The animal was so crazed with anger that it destroyed the crops, and no one could approach it.

Heracles chased the Boar up to the snowy peak of Mt. Erymanthus, lassoed it and picked it up on his shoulders. When he arrived back at Mycenae, Eurystheus was so scared he hid in a storage jar for olive oil.

When Heracles brought the Erymanthian boar to Mycenae, the terrified King Eurystheus hid in a pithos. (Athenian black-figure amphora, middle 6th cent. BC.

The Stymphalian Birds

These were birds which lived in a dense forest on the banks of Lake Stymphalia, in Arcadia. They were predators with wings of steel so sharp that they whistled over the heads of their enemies like knife blades. They had become a real scourge in the area, devouring all the fruit and destroying the crops. Eurystheus ordered Heracles to exterminate them. The major problem was getting the birds out of the forest, which was too dense to hunt them in. The goddess Athena gave Heracles a set of bronze rattles made by Hephaestus, with which he was able to scare the birds and then shoot them with his arrows. Those that survived had been frightened so badly that they flew away and never troubled Lake Stymphalia again.

Hercales fights to drive off the Stymphalian Birds. (Beginning of the 5th century BC, black-figure amphora, the Louvre, Paris).

The Augean Stables

Heracles cleaning the Augean Stables. (475 BC, metope from the Temple of Zeus at Olympia, Archaeological Museum of Olympia).

Augeas, son of Helios, was the king of Elis in the Peloponnese. He had vast herds of cattle, but had been remiss in cleaning out their stables, thus creating two huge problems for his country: on the one hand, the soil was becoming infertile because no manure was being spread on it, and on the other the accumulated filth was in danger of polluting all of Elis. Heracles hit upon a simple but clever way of performing the work. After digging a channel into the foundations of the stables he was able to change the course of the Peneus and Alpheus rivers whose currents swept out the dung and deposited it on the farmlands of Elis.

The Horses of Diomedes

Part of the 1st century AD frieze in the museum of Delphi showing Heracles and the Horses of Diomedes.

Diomedes was a Thracian king who possessed a herd of man-eating horses nourished on the flesh of unfortunate passersby. Eurystheus dispatched Heracles to Thrace to bring the horses back to Mycenae.

The hero accomplished his labour, although he had to feed Diomedes himself to the horses to do it. After eating their master, the horses calmed down and obediently followed Heracles.

The Cretan Bull

Heracles taming the Cretan Bull. (5th century BC, metope from the Temple of Zeus at Olympia).

The Cretan Bull was a magnificent animal which emerged from the waves in response to a promise by Minos, king of Crete, that he would sacrifice to Poseidon anything that came out of the sea. But the bull was so handsome that Minos could not bring himself to sacrifice it, so he put it among his herd and sacrificed another bull in its place. Poseidon, they say, took his revenge by filling the bull with such madness that it snorted fire from its nostrils. Eurystheus assigned Heracles the task of bringing him the bull alive. Heracles asked Minos for help, but all the king would do was allow him to capture the animal. Heracles eventually caught it alive and returned to the Argolid riding on its back as it swam.

The Girdle of Queen Hippolyta

O ne day it occurred to Admete, daughter of king Eurystheus, that she would like to have the girdle of Hippolyta, queen of the Amazons, and so Heracles received his orders to leave the country on this errand.

The Amazons were a warlike race composed entirely of women. Of the children to whom they gave birth, they allowed only the girls to live, cutting off their right breasts when they grew up so as not to obstruct their archery. They were excellent horsewomen and skilled in the arts of war, and men approached them at their peril. Hippolyta, their queen, wore a unique belt of gold and precious stones, a gift from her father the war-god Ares, as her emblem of authority. After many adventures and battles, Heracles and his companions managed to take the belt.

The Oxen of Geryon

T he demi-god's next labour was to bring to Mycenae the Oxen of Geryon, and this adventure took him to the island of Eurytheia, at the end of the West. The monstrous Geryon from the waist up had three bodies - that is, six arms and three heads. He is also said to have had wings. As soon as he landed on Eurytheia, Heracles killed Orthros (who sprang at him) with his club and then finished off Eurytion. Then he was able to seize the valuable oxen and sail away. There are a number of tales about the feats Heracles performed during the voyage. As he sailed by, he is said to have killed various monsters and robbers who haunted the coasts of Libya and Africa. To commemorate the fact that he had been at Tartessus, he built two columns, known as the Pillars of Heracles, one on either side of what is now called the Straits of Gibraltar which separate Europe from Africa.

Heracles killing the attendants of the Egyptian king Busiris at the altar. This event, as well as many others, occurred during his campaign to the west. (470 BC, National Archaeological Museum of Athens).

Heracles struggling with Antaeus who is immobilized in the hero's grip. (510 - 500 BC, red-figure krater, the Louvre, Paris).

The Golden Apples of the Hesperides

F ar away to the west of Libya, in the foothills, perhaps, of the Atlas Mountains, was once found the Garden of the Hesperides, with its trees of golden apples. The daughters of Atlas were forever trespassing in the garden and stealing the apples, so Hera gave the task of guarding them to an immortal dragon with a hundred heads, assisted by the three Nymphs called the Hesperides.

Although he did all he could to extract from the god Nereus the exact route he should follow, Heracles still had many adventures on the way. One of them involved wrestling with the giant Antaeus. This was far from easy, since as long as the giant had his feet on the ground he could draw strength from Earth, his mother. Heracles realised this and, with a superhuman effort, managed to lift Antaeus on to his shoulders, breaking his contact with the ground. Then he could squeeze him in his arms in mid-air and throttle him. On this voyage, among other perigrinations, Heracles freed Prometheus, the benefactor of mankind, whom Zeus had condemned to be chained to the Caucasus Mountains for giving mankind fire and breaking the rule which restricted its use to the gods alone. The eagle that tore at Prometheus' vitals, dropped dead from Heracles' arrow.

The Giant Atlas was responsible for holding up the sky on his shoulders. Heracles offered to relieve him of his burden for a while, on condition that Atlas went and picked three golden apples from the Garden of the Hesperides.

Atlas fetched the apples, but was then unwilling to resume his burden, offering instead to take the precious fruit to Eurystheus. Once again, the demi-god was forced to use all his cunning: he asked Atlas to hold up the dome of the heavens for a moment while he, unused to such weights, put a cushion on his shoulders. Atlas, unsuspecting, shouldered the burden - only to discover that Heracles had snatched up the apples which Atlas had laid down and taken to his heels.

Eurystheus got his apples, but did not know what to do with them. So he gave them to Athena, who took them back to the Garden; such fruit, she knew, should not be kept anywhere but in a divine garden.

Cerberus

T his labour differs from all of Heracles' others because it involves the desecration of a sacred place and violation of the laws of nature. As the supreme feat, Eurystheus asked Heracles to bring him the guard-dog of the underworld.

Pluto gave his consent for Heracles to take Cerberus away with him, on condition that he could tame the animal without weapons, wearing only his breast-plate and lion-skin. So Heracles wrestled with the dog, clutching him tightly despite the wounds caused by the animal's lashing tail, until it gave in.

When he took the dog back to Mycenae, Eurytheus hid in his storage jar again, out of fear, and since there seemed little else to do with Cerberus, Heracles took him back to Hades where he belonged.

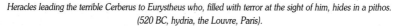

Heracles leading the terrible Cerberus to Eurystheus who, filled with terror at the sight of him, hides in a pithos.
(520 BC, hydria, the Louvre, Paris).

The death and deification of Heracles

Heracles accomplished many more feats and labours during his lifetime. He served on campaigns, made war and dispatched numerous robbers and wild beasts. There are countless narratives and legends in which these doings can be found in various forms. But the hero's death is associated with his fatal marriage to Deianeira, a match which he had decided on during his descent into Hades, where he met her brother Meleager and promised to marry his sister. That agreement, made in a place like the underworld, proved to be decisive. It so happened that when travelling together, Heracles and Deianeira had to cross the river Euenus, where the ferryman was the Centaur Nessus, who lived nearby. Nessus rowed Heracles across first, and then came back for Deianeira. He attempted to ravish her - but Heracles, hearing her cries from the opposite bank, fitted an arrow to his bow and wounded the Centaur in the heart. Nessus decided to take his revenge. He told Deianeira that if she wanted to have Heracles with her forever, should she ever be afraid of losing him, she should make a magic potion out of the blood trickling from his wound.

Deianeira believed him, collected some of the Centaur's blood, and took it with her. Some time later, Heracles was victorious over Eurytus in the conquest of Oechalia. Wishing to erect an altar to Zeus and sacrifice to him, he sent his comrade Lichas to Trachis, where Deianeira was then living, to fetch him clean new clothes for the ceremony. Deianeira was afraid that the company of Iole, daughter of Eurytus, whom Heracles had taken as his concubine, might drive his lawful wife from his mind, and so she dipped his new tunic in the blood of Nessus. Heracles put it on and began the sacrifice. But the poison in the Centaur's blood soon burned his skin. Heracles tried to tear off the poisoned tunic, but his flesh came away with it. When Deianeira realised what she had done, she committed suicide. Then Heracles climbed to the top of Mt Oete, where he built a pyre and ordered his friends to set fire both to it and him. All were reluctant to obey him, and only Philoctetes had the courage to start the fire. In gratitude, Heracles gave Philoctetes his bow and the arrows soaked in the blood of the Lernaean Hydra.

When the flames had begun to rise high, thunder was heard, lightning flashed and a cloud descended to take Heracles into the sky. So it came about that he joined the immortals and ascended to Olympus, where he married Hebe, the goddess of eternal youth.

*Heracles on a Roman copy of a Greek original from the
5th century BC. (Museum of Naples).*

THESEUS

Aegeas asks for a prophecy from the oracle. (440 - 430 BC, interior of a red-figure kylix).

Theseus is the hero of Athens, and he occupies a position equivalent to that of Heracles for the Dorians, although he is a generation younger. His father was Aegeas, king of Athens, and his mother was Aethra, daughter of king Pittheus of Troezen. However, in many versions his true father is Poseidon, and there are numerous myths surrounding his birth. The best-known relates how after two barren marriages Aegeas sent to the Delphic Oracle for advice. The oracle told him not to untie the mouth of his wineskin before he returned to Athens lest one day he should die of grief. Unable to understand the words of the oracle, Aegeas decided to travel home via Troezen, to consult king Pittheus, who was known for his wisdom. Whether Pittheus understood the oracle or not, he wanted his daughter to be the mother of the son whom the king of Athens wished for so dearly. He arranged a great feast at which Aegeas drank deeply of the wine, after which Pittheus saw to it that he spent the night with Aethra. Waking in the morning next to the beautiful Aethra, Aegeas left her his sword and sandals, over which he rolled an enormous boulder. He left instructions that if the boy to be born was so strong that he could lift the boulder and take his father's sandals and sword, he was to be put them on and come to Athens. The sandals and sword would be the sign by which Aegeas would recognise him.

The boyhood of Theseus

Theseus grew up in Troezen with his mother and grandfather, and was a strong, handsome child.

When he reached the age of sixteen, his mother thought he was strong enough to embark upon the next stage in his life. She revealed his paternity to him, and took him to the boulder. Theseus easily rolled it away, found his father's sandals and sword, put them on and prepared to leave for Athens. In vain Aethra and Pittheus implored him to go by sea and not by the land route, which at that time was infested with robbers and wild beasts. But Theseus, envying the glory of Heracles, was thirsty for heroic feats, and had made up his mind to travel by land.

Following his mother's instructions, Theseus moves the rock and finds his father's sword and sandals. (1st century AD, Roman terracotta relief, British Museum, London).

The road to Athens

T he first robber whom Theseus encountered, in the vicinity of
   Epidaurus, was called Periphetes. He lay in wait for
passing travellers and killed them with a huge metal club.
Theseus took his club away from him and killed him
with. As he approached Cechreae, a second and
equally dangerous opponent hove in sight. This
was Sines Pityocamptes, which means
"pine-bender", a son of Poseidon. Sines
killed strangers in a particularly gruesome
manner: he pulled down the tops of two
adjacent pine trees, to each of which he
tied one leg of the unfortunate
traveller. Then he let the trees spring
apart again, ripping his victim in
two. Theseus' punishment of Sines
was to put him to death in the
same way.

Theseus continued his journey
and entered Corinthian territory,
where he fought with spear and
sword against a fearful beast of
the underworld, a wild sow
which belonged to an old woman
called Phaea or Crommyo - a name
taken from Crommyum, the place
where she lived. The next stage of his
travels took Theseus into the kingdom of
Megara and to the most dangerous point on
his journey, the section of the road beneath
the Geranian Mountains (now known as the
"Bad Step"). Here the road was merely a narrow
path barely wide enough for one traveller. On the
one side were the precipitous slopes of the mountain,
and on the other was a steep drop into the sea, just like
today. The coastline was the haunt of a wild carnivorous turtle,
which devoured all those who approached. High up on the cliffs, the
pass was controlled by Sciron, a robber who made passers by wash his feet -
supposedly in return for allowing them to travel on. While they were at their task,
he would kick them down the cliff into the sea, where the turtle ate them.

However, the gods had so arranged things that it was Sciron's fate to die in the same way. Theseus threw him down from on high, and the turtle devoured him.

One of Theseus' most renowned exploits was his punishment of the robber Procrustes, the next obstacle on his journey. This unusual robber killed his victims and took their belongings after first forcing them to lie down on his awful bed. If the poor traveller was taller than the bed was long, Procrustes cut off the extra length of leg. If, on the other hand, he was too short, the robber tied ropes to his arms and legs and stretched him till he fitted the bed. In fact, it is said that Procrustes had two beds for this purpose: a short one for tall people, and a long one for the short. Theseus dealt with him in the way he had dealt with so many. As a result, the reputation of Theseus arrived in Athens before he did. At this time, Aegeas had just married the sorceress Medea. She knew in advance who Theseus was as he progressed towards Athens. Without giving away any details to the king, she managed to inspire in him a fear of the young hero, whose beauty had already become legendary. She managed to convince Aegeas to offer Theseus a poisoned drink. But as the youth went to cut a piece off the sacrificial animal with his sword - perhaps intentionally - Aegeas recognised the weapon and then the sandals which Theseus was wearing. He sprang forward and stopped him from raising the poisoned cup, recognising as he did so his son. Aegeas poured out the contents of the cup and exiled Medea from his country.

Representations of the exploits of Theseus. In the centre the hero has already deafeated the Minotaur. To the right, Theseus raises a lekani against Sciron below whom the turtle is visible. Next are shown the capture of the Bull of Marathon, the punishment of Sinis, the slaying of the sow Phaea, the battle with Cercyon, and finally the punishment of Procrustes. (440 - 430 BC, interior of a red-figure kylix, British Museum, London).

The Cretan Cycle

A ndrogeos, son of Minos, was a charismatic young
man and outstanding athlete who came to Athens in
order to compete in games organised by Aegeas. The
young prince from Crete succeeded in beating all the other
competitors. Envious of his success, Aegeas sent him
against the bull of Marathon, which slew Androgeos.

The news of the death of his son reached Minos as he
was sacrificing on Paros. As soon as the feast was over, he
summoned his fleet and sailed to attack Athens. The war
lasted some time and ended with the defeat of Athens,
which Minos compelled to pay him a tribute of blood: each
year, seven youths and seven maidens were sent to Crete
and fed to the monstrous Minotaur. The Minotaur was a
monster with a human body and the head of a bull. He was
the son of Pasiphae, the wife of Minos and a bull that
Poseidon had sent to Minos. Minos, shamed by the birth of
this monster, called on the architect Daedalus to build the
Labyrinth as a palace in which the terrible Minotaur was
incarcerated and fed on human bodies. Before long,
Theseus had to deal with this problem when the time came
to send the annual 'tribute' to Minos.

Thus, he decided that he would be one of the seven
youths sent to the Minotaur - in the hope that he could kill
the beast. When the party set out for Crete, their ship had
black sails, indicative of its melancholy mission. But Aegeas
had given them white sails as well, which they were to
hoist if they returned in joy and triumph. The white sails
would signal the news of their victory even before the ship
docked. Theseus arrived in Crete, and was led to the
Labyrinth with the others.

Representation of the labyrinth where Theseus slew the Minotaur.
(Roman mosaic of the 4th century BC,
Museum of Art, Vienna).

But Ariadne, daughter of Minos, saw him and fell in love with him. Before the youths entered the palace, she had time to give him a ball of thread, telling him to tie one end to the entrance of the Labyrinth and unwind it as he went, so that he could find his way back.

She also made Theseus promise to take her back to Athens with him and marry her. Theseus killed the Minotaur with his bare fists, liberated his companions and managed to flee in secret from Crete, taking Ariadne with him. But when the ship stopped at the island of Naxos on the way back to Athens, Theseus left Ariadne there, to be consoled by the god Dionysus. Although everything had gone well, the happy returning travellers forgot to hoist their white sails in place of the black ones. Poor king Aegeas, watching from the peak of Cape Sounion, saw the ship with its black sails, concluded that his son was dead, and threw himself to his death off the cliff into the sea which ever since has been called the Aegean.

Theseus slays the Minotaur. (Black-figure amphora, the Louvre, Paris).

The kingdom and the death of Theseus

Theseus proved to be a good king. He made Athens the capital of his state, established social classes, minted coins and established the Panathenaea as the festival which symbolised the political unity of Attica. He fought off the Amazons when they attacked Athens. He lived many years, married Phaedra, and accomplished numerous feats - including escaping from imprisonment in the underworld, with the help of Heracles. In his later years, he formed a close friendship with the hero Perithoos. Once, though, he went to visit his kinsman king Lycomedes of Skyros, who took him up on to a high cliff, supposedly to admire the view of the island to be had from there. Lycomedes treacherously pushed Theseus off the cliff and killed him.

His remains were found during historical times by the general Kimon and transported back to Athens and accorded a funeral worthy of this great Attic hero.

THE VOYAGE OF THE ARGONAUTS

The campaign of the Greeks to Colchis under the leadership of Jason was one of the most important events of mythical times because the finest young men in Greece took part in it. But let us speak of the events that led up to this great campaign.

Phrixos and Helle

A thamas, the king of Orchomenos in Boeotia, had two children by his wife Nephele: Phrixos and Helle. But Ino seduced the king and persuaded him to drive out Nephele and take her as his wife. Ino was a bad stepmother to the children. Her hate for them caused her to lay the following plan.

She persuaded the women of the country to bake the seed-corn stored for the next planting. Naturally enough, the baked seed failed to sprout when planted, and so famine struck the country.

Athamas sent envoys to the Delphic Oracle to ask the god what he should do. Ino bribed the envoys to say that the oracle had told them Phrixos would have to be sacrificed to Zeus before the earth would bring forth fruit. The people rose up in anger, demanding that the king obey the oracle. Athamas had to give in, but just as Phrixos was being led to the sacrificial altar Nephele, the children's mother, sent a ram with a golden fleece.

Phrixos and Helle mounted the ram and it flew off. As they crossed the Thracian peninsula, however, Helle looked down, became giddy and fell. She drowned in the waters of the strait known since then as the Hellespont. Phrixos arrived alone in Colchis, where the king was Aeetes, son of Helios and Perseis and brother of the sorceress Circe.

Holding onto the horns of the ram, Phrixos flies over the sea heading for Colchis. (Circa 460 BC, red-figure pelike, National Archaeological Museum of Athens).

There he sacrificed the ram to Zeus, in gratitude, and begged the protection of Aeetes, who made him his son-in-law. Phrixos, in turn, gave the king the golden fleece. Aeetes hung the fleece on an oak tree in a grove sacred to the god Ares and set a dragon which never slept to guard it night and day.

All the Centaurs, except for Pholus and Chiron, had a wild character.
Here, two Centaurs are beating Pirithous, king of the Lapiths,
with saplings because he had overstepped the bounds the gods had defined for men.

Pelias and Jason

The king of Iolkos was Pelias, son of Poseidon and Tyro, who had usurped the throne from his halfbrother Aeson. Afraid that Pelias would kill his son Jason, the rightful heir to the throne, Aeson took him to the cave of the Centaur Chiron, on Mt. Pelion, to whom he assigned the task up bringing the boy up. The wise Chiron taught Jason the learning and arts of the age, and when he was old enough set him on the road to Iolkos to claim his throne. So when Jason, demanded the throne that was his by right, his crafty uncle claimed that he had had a dream in which Phrixos begged him to do something to bring his spirit home, along with the golden fleece from the palace of king Aeetes in Colchis. And so he asked the young Jason to do as this oracular pronouncement required: to build a ship and set out. In other words, Jason was to undertake the task of putting the soul of Phrixos to rest. Pelias promised and swore in the name of the gods that as soon as Jason returned with the golden fleece to Iolkos he would surrender the throne to him.

Preparations for the Journey

J ason agreed to Pelias' terms and began to prepare for the voyage. He commissioned the architect and shipbuilder Argos to build him a vessel with fifty oars. Once finished, the ship was far superior to any other of its time. It was also very speedy, which was why it was called Argo (argos = quick).

While the Argo was being made ready, Chiron advised Jason to have heralds travel throughout Greece spreading the word of his long journey and inviting brave and noble youths to take part in the campaign. And so Jason did: and the crew of his ship, the Argonauts as they were called, were all heroes or even the sons of gods. They included Tiphes (helmsman of the Argo), Orpheus the musician, the soothsayers Idmon and Mopsus, Heracles, Hylas, Idas, Castor and Pollux, Periclymenus (son of Neleus), Peleas and his brother Telamon, and many others who made up the flower of the young generation of the day.

Preparations for the voyage of the Argo under the supervision of the goddess Athena.
(First half of the 1st century AD, British Museum, London).

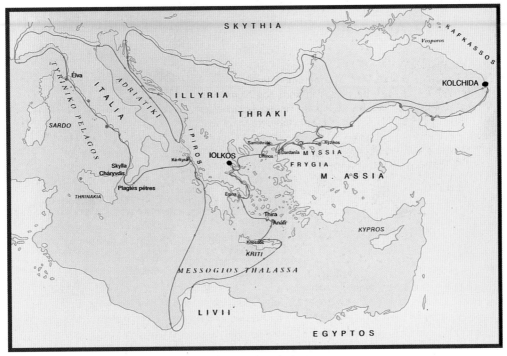

The voyage of the Argo, according to the description by Apollonius of Rhodes in the 'Argonautica'.

The Voyage of the Argo

After sacrificing to Apollo, the Argonauts embarked in the port of Pagasae. The omens for the voyage were good, and the ship set off. The first stop on their way was Lemnos, where they found the island women husbandless: all the men had been killed. The Argonauts formed unions with the women and helped them bear sons before sailing. After calling at Samothrace, they entered the Hellespont and reached Cyzicus. The king of the land, also called Cyzicus, and his people, the Doliani, made the travellers very welcome. But when they tried to sail on, a head wind drove them back - and by a fatal misunderstanding, they failed to recognise the Doliani and the Doliani did not recognise them. There was a fierce battle in which Cyzicus and his subjects were massacred by the Argonauts. When they realised their mistake, it was too late, but each side, regretting what had happened, honoured the dead of the other.

On the coast of Mysia, their next stop, the Nymphs abducted Hylas, beloved friend of Heracles. Heracles stayed on there with Polyphemus to search for his friend and the rest of the company departed without them. Arriving in the country of the soothsayer Phineas, they freed him from the terrible Harpies, in return for which he revealed the future to them and told them how to deal with the Symplegades, the Clashing Rocks. The Symplegades were rocks which suddenly clashed together, crushing any ship which might happen to be passing between them at the time. Phineas told the Argonauts to release a dove and let it fly between

The Argonauts persuing the terrible Harpes –Aello, Ocypete and Celaeno– who were torturing the seer Phineus. (570 BC, ivory relief figures from a Corinthian workshop, Archaeological Museum of Delphi).

the Symplegades first. If it managed to get through, then they would be able to follow it; if not, they were to hold back. Sure enough, the Argonauts released a dove and it flew through the gap, the Clashing Rocks managing only to knock a few feathers out of its tail. The Argo was similarly fortunate: it sailed between the rocks and escaped only with slight damage to its stern. In the end, after still more adventures, the Argo and her crew arrived in the country of king Aeetes.

In Colchis

A s soon as the company arrived in Colchis, Jason presented himself before king Aeetes and told him of the orders he had received from Pelias. Aeetes declared his willingness to part with the golden fleece - on condition that without any assistance Jason yoked two bulls given him by Hephaestus, which had bronze hooves and breathed fire, and then used them to plough a field and sow it with dragon's teeth, which he would provide.

With the help of Medea, Jason managed to accomplish the feat. But Aeetes did not keep his word, and even tried to burn the Argo and kill the Argonauts. So Jason - once again with the help of Medea - put the dragon to sleep, stole the golden fleece, and set sail with all possible speed.

As soon as Aeetes discovered that Jason and Medea had fled - taking with them the golden fleece - he set off in pursuit of the Argo. In order to delay him, Medea killed her brother Apsyrtus (who had accompanied them) and, every so often, threw a part of his body into the sea.

The unfortunate Aeetes lost time by stopping to collect the pieces of his beloved son, and soon the fugitives were out of danger.

Medea helping the hero to achieve his goal. She diverts the attention of the dragon offering him a sleeping potion while, at the same time, Jason manages to remove the golden fleece which is hanging on the branch of a tree. (Beginning of the 4th century BC, Archaeological Museum of Naples).

The Return to Ioklos

T he Argo wandered about a great deal, experiencing many dangers and bad weather, eventually coming home to Iolkos, bearing with them the priceless golden fleece. Now the time had come for Jason to lay claim to the throne of King Pelias. But Pelias - who in the meantime had put all of Jason's relatives to death - refused to give up the throne to the rightful heir. So Jason was forced to resort to the magical powers and cunning of the witch Medea. She managed to gain entrance to the palace and set Pelias' daughters to kill him, tricking them into thinking they were taking part in a rite to rejuvenate their father. From this point on, we find a number of variations of the myth. In one, Jason and Medea ruled Iolkos and entrusted the son born to them to the Centaur Chiron; in another, they left the city and went to live in Corinth, after putting Acastus, Pelias' only son, on the throne.

Jason, with the golden fleece in his hands, returns to Iolcos where Pelias welcomes him.
(350 - 340 BC, Apulian krater, the Louvre, Paris).

PERSEUS

P erseus, son of Zeus and Danae, was a hero of Argòs. His grandfather, Acrisius, once asked an oracle if he would ever have sons. The oracle replied that it would be the destiny of his daughter Danae to have a son who would kill him. In order to prevent this

prophecy from coming true, Acrisius had Danae shut up in an underground cave with brass walls. But Zeus managed to squeeze through a crack in the cave - after transforming himself into a shower of golden rain - and formed a union with the lovely Danae.

She gave birth to a son, whom she managed to bring up in secret for some months. When Acrisius found out about the baby, he refused to believe that Zeus had had anything to do with it; he killed Danae's wet-nurse, whom he suspected of complicity in the affair, and put his daughter and grandson in a wooden

Acrisius gives directions to his carpenter for the chest in which he plans to place Danae and the newborn Perseus. (Circa 490 BC, red-figure hydria).

ark and set them adrift on the sea. The waves washed them up on Seriphos, where the fisherman Dictes, brother of Polydectes, tyrant of the island, found it. Dictes took in Perseus and his mother, and it was in his house that the boy grew into a brave young man blessed with talents and gifts of all kinds. At one point King Polydectes fell in love with Danae, but he was never able to meet her because Perseus kept his mother well-guarded and the king felt unable to bring pressure to bear. Once, Polydectes invited Perseus to dinner with some other friends, and asked them what gifts they would give him if the need arose. All the young men

answered that a horse was the most suitable gift for a king. Only Perseus answered that if it was absolutely necessary he would bring Polydectes the head of Medusa, the Gorgon. Polydectes pounced on this promise to demand that Perseus bring him the head of Medusa - otherwise, he said, he would seize Danae by force. And so Perseus set out to find the Gorgon and cut off her head.

Perseus has already decapitated Medusa and is on his way back. Athena, his guardian, stands close to the dying Gorgon. (Circa 460 BC, red-figure hydria).

Perseus' feat and Perseus' revenge

Athena and Hermes helped Perseus accomplish his feat. By a cunning trick, he managed to get the Nymphs to lend him winged sandals, a bag, and the helmet of Hades which would make him invisible. Hermes gave him a razor-sharp sickle. When Perseus came upon the Gorgons, they were asleep. Using the winged sandals, he swooped up high and cut off Medusa's head while looking at her reflection in the shiny shield which Athena had given him: if he had looked her straight in the eye, she would have turned him to stone. As soon as Medusa's head was off, Pegasus and the giant Chrysaor sprang from her neck. Perseus put the head in the bag and set off for home. Medusa's two sisters chased him, but in vain: wearing the helmet of Hades, Perseus was invisible.

Perseus and the Graeae. (Circa 425 BC, lid of a pyxis, National Archaeological Museum of Athens).

Perseus and Medusa. The winged horse, Pegasus, is shown next to his mother, Medusa, while Athena stands on the left. The distribution of the forward-facing figures is characteristic of Archaic art. (Middle of the 6th century BC, metope from a limestone sculpture of a Greek temple in Sicily).

On his way back, Perseus met Andromeda, a beautiful maiden whom he saved from the chains which bound her to a rock and the sea monster which was on the point of devouring her. Andromeda's parents agreed to a marriage between their daughter and her saviour, but Phineas, her uncle (who had been planning to wed her himself), began to plot against Perseus. As soon as Perseus realised what was going on, he produced the head of Medusa and turned Phineas and his fellow conspirators to stone.

When Perseus got back to Seriphos, he took the same revenge on Polydectes, who, he was told, had been subjecting Danae to insufferable pressure. Once Polydectes and his cronies had been turned to statues, Perseus put his adoptive father Dictes on the throne and, taking Andromeda with him, set out for Argos, his home, to meet his grandfather. But as soon as Acrisius heard of the approach of his grandson, he fled - yet he did not escape his fate. Later, he was present as a spectator at games in Larisa arranged by King Tentamides, at which Perseus was a competitor in the discus. When Perseus' turn came to throw, the discus slipped from his hand and hit Acrisius on the head, killing him. Perseus was grieved to learn who the dead man had been, and buried him with every honour.

The Gorgon with a 'belt' of snakes. (Circa 590 BC, from the pediment of the Temple of Artemis, Archaeological Museum of Corfu).

Head of Medusa.
Detail from a floor mosaic
of the Late Helladic period.

BELLEROPHON

B ellerophon was actually the son of Poseidon, but among men his father was taken to be Glaucus, son of Sisyphus. His mother was Eurynome, daughter of King Nisus of Megara. This hero acquired his name after killing a tyrant of Corinth called Bellerus.

After the murder, he was forced to leave Corinth and seek out King Proetus of Tiryns, to expiate his crime. But when he was staying there Anteia, the wife of Proetus, fell in love with the young and handsome penitent - who denied her, out of respect for her husband's hospitality. To revenge this slight, Anteia went to Proetus and accused Bellerophon of having tried to seduce her, demanding that her husband put him to death.

Terracotta tablet showing Bellerophon slaying the Chimera. (660 BC, Archaeological Museum of Thassos).

Proetus decided to send Bellerophon - who, we should remember, was the owner of the winged horse Pegasus - to his father-in-law Iobates in Lycia, since he himself was prevented by the unwritten laws of hospitality from killing the youth. Iobates welcomed Bellerophon with feasting, and declared nine days of celebrations in his honour, during which time he sacrificed nine bulls as part of the rites in honour of his guest. On the tenth day he opened the letter from his son-in-law. It occurred to him, when he read Iobates' request that Bellerophon be put to death, that he could ask him instead to kill the Chimera. Bellerophon agreed to undertake the task. His greatest difficulty was with the fiery breath of the Chimera, which could throw its flames a considerable distance. But here he was helped by Pegasus, who soared up high with his rider and allowed Bellerophon to shoot the Chimera with his arrows from a safe distance.

After the Chimera had been dealt with, Iobates next commanded that Bellerophon be sent to fight the people called the Solymi, a fierce and belligerent tribe. Once they had been annihilated, the next order was to fight the Amazons. They, too, were

Fragment of a terracotta akroterion showing Bellerophon astride Pegasus. (540 - 500 BC, Archaeological Museum of Thassos).

defeated. Iobates was nearing despair, and his last attempt to kill Bellerophon consisted of the formation of a crack unit of troops whom he set to lie in ambush for the hero. But Bellerophon beat them, just as he had all the others. These feats convinced Iobates that Bellerophon must be of divine descent. He disclosed the instructions that Proetus had sent him, and out of respect and admiration for Bellerophon kept him by his side, married him to his daughter and, later, left him his kingdom.

Bellerophon met his end much later, we are told. His arrogance became such that he decided to fly up to the summit of Olympus on his winged steed, to see the house of Zeus and perhaps even take part in the councils of the gods. But Zeus was enraged by the hero's vanity, and Pegasus, the divine horse, threw his rider from the peak of the mountain. Then he returned to Olympus, where his true place was. From then on, he served Zeus by bringing him thunderbolts and helped Io (the Dawn) when the time came for the day to break.

Bellerophon astride Pegasus. (End of the 5th century BC, National Archaeological Museum of Athens).

DAEDALUS AND ICARUS

The Athenian craftsman Daedalus was a member of the royal family of Cecrops, first king of Athens. He was an artist of the greatest importance: he produced sculptures, works of architecture and some of the greatest inventions of his day. But for all his talents, the master craftsman was exiled for having committed a crime.

And so Daedalus found himself in the service of King Minos of Crete, for whom, among other marvels he constructed the famous Labyrinth, a palace whose corridors were so complicated that it was impossible to retain one's bearings. It was in this maze that Minos enclosed the Minotaur. While living in Crete, Daedalus had a son, Icarus, with a slave-woman in the palace, named Naucrate. When Theseus came to Crete in order to kill the Minotaur, it was Daedalus who showed Ariadne how best to advise the hero on entering and leaving the Labyrinth. When Minos found out what he had done, he was so furious that he shut the artist and his son up in the Labyrinth themselves. There, in prison, Daedalus never ceased to think about ways in which he could escape from Crete. One day the thought of wings struck him. He stuck the feathers together with wax and fitted them to the shoulders of himself and Icarus, and the two set off on their incredible journey. But young Icarus was deaf to his father's advice: Daedalus had told him not to fly too low in case his wings touched the wave-crests and got wet, or too high, as the sun would get them too hot. But Icarus, in his arrogance, flew higher and higher - until the wax in his wings melted in the heat of the sun and he plunged into the sea. That part of the ocean has ever since been called the Icarian Sea. Icarus' body was washed ashore on an island called Icaria since that time, and Heracles found it and buried it.

The multifaceted and inventive talents of Daedalus enabled him to construct the wings that would allow him and his son to fly far away from their prison and become the first people 'in the air'.

The fall of Icarus, from a wall painting in Pompeii (Naples, National Museum, 10 BC).

ORPHEUS

O rpheus of Thrace was one of the protagonists in the Argonaut adventure. He is also the central figure in a highly symbolic myth with more religious features about it than any other of its time. The son of Oeagrus and (probably) the Muse Calliope, Orpheus was a charismatic musician, poet and singer. Apart from being a superb performer on the lyre, he was credited with inventing the cithara, the ancient guitar.

The most familiar myth about Orpheus is that which tells of his descent into Hades in search of his beloved wife Eurydice. It goes as follows. Eurydice was a beautiful nymph of the woods. One day, she was running away from the attentions of Aristaeus, along the bank of a river, when she trod on a poisonous snake. It bit her and she died. Orpheus, inconsolable, descended into Hades to find her and bring her back to life. His music charmed the entire Underworld, and all the souls in torment there forgot their punishments for a little while. Sisyphus, Tantalus, the Danaids and all the others rested from their eternal tortures to listen with delight to the music. Hades and Persephone agreed to let Eurydice go, but on one condition: that as Orpheus was ascending to the upper world once more, with Eurydice behind him, he must not turn round to look at her until they were safely out of the Underworld. But just before they emerged into the sunlight, Orpheus' anxiety to make sure that the shade of Eurydice really was behind him overcame him, and he turned round to make absolutely sure the gods of the underworld had not tricked him. Then everything was lost for ever; Eurydice joined the dead with no hope of return, and Hades turned a deaf ear to the pleas of the tragic figure of Orpheus. After that time, there are many tales of Orpheus the inconsolable widower. He is said to have turned his back on worldly things, of refusing to remarry, of avoiding women and their love for three years.

According to tradition, his only companions were Thracian boys, to whom he taught the 'Orphic life': abstinence from the consumpfion of meat, and initiation into music and the experiences which Orpheus himself had had in the underworld.

As for the death of Orpheus, the myths tell us that he became involved in a succession of relationships with men. This provoked the women whom he had spurned since the death of Eurydice to a frenzy of revenge. The Muses buried his remains and wept for him.

Orpheus' end approaches as a woman attacks him with her sword.
(450 - 440 BC, red-figure amphora, the Louvre, Paris).

Orpheus and the animals. The magic of Orpheus' music tamed the wild beasts.

The brilliant god Helios,
with his chariot which he agreed to give for a short while to his son Phaethon.
(435 BC, red-figure krater, British Museum, London).

PHAETHON

There are many stories about Phaethon, son of Helios the sun-god. When Phaethon reached adolescence he asked his father to let him drive the chariot of the sun. Helios refused, at first, but eventually gave in, bombarding the young man with instructions and advice.

To begin with, Phaethon took the route Helios used every day, but when he had gained height he took fright at the drop beneath him. The proximity to the signs of the Zodiac scared him, too, and he changed course. The chariot began to veer wildly about the sky, sometimes coming so low it was in danger of setting fire to the earth, and sometimes soaring so high it nearly scorched the stars. To put an end to this menace, Zeus let loose a thunderbolt and shot Phaethon down into the river Eridanus, where his sisters, the Heliads, buried him with all the honours due to the dead.

THE ROYAL HOUSE OF THE LABDACIDS

The royal house of the Labdacids, named after Labdacus, the grandson of Cadmus (who was the founder of Thebes) held a special place in the Theban Cycle. Oedipus, the dominant figure in the family, along with its other members, have come to create classical characters by means of their adventures.

OEDIPUS

Laius, the king of Thebes, married Jocasta, daughter of Menoiceus and sister of Creon. Time passed, however, and Laius and Jocaste had had no sons. So the king went to the oracle, as was the custom then. The oracle told him that the couple would indeed have a son, but that he would bring great misfortune upon Thebes, killing the king, his father, and marrying his mother.

Oedipus solving the riddle of the Sphinx. (470 - 460 BC, interior of a red-figure kylix, Vatican Museum, Rome).

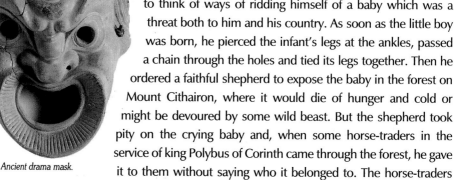

Ancient drama mask.

After that, Laius kept well away from his wife. But Jocasta wanted a child more than anything else in the world, and so she got Laius drunk at a feast and spent the night with him. As soon as he discovered that the queen was with child, Laius began to think of ways of ridding himself of a baby which was a threat both to him and his country. As soon as the little boy was born, he pierced the infant's legs at the ankles, passed a chain through the holes and tied its legs together. Then he ordered a faithful shepherd to expose the baby in the forest on Mount Cithairon, where it would die of hunger and cold or might be devoured by some wild beast. But the shepherd took pity on the crying baby and, when some horse-traders in the service of king Polybus of Corinth came through the forest, he gave it to them without saying who it belonged to. The horse-traders took the baby to Polybus and his wife, who - childless themselves - were only too glad to look after it. Queen Merope gave the boy the name Oedipus, which means 'swollen-footed', because his legs had swelled up where Laius had pierced them to put on the chains.

The grave monument shown in this scene represents Oedipus. Antigone approaches the tomb with an offering, while a young man (possibly Polynices or Eteocles) also approaches offering a garland. (4th century BC, Lucanian amphora, the Louvre, Paris).

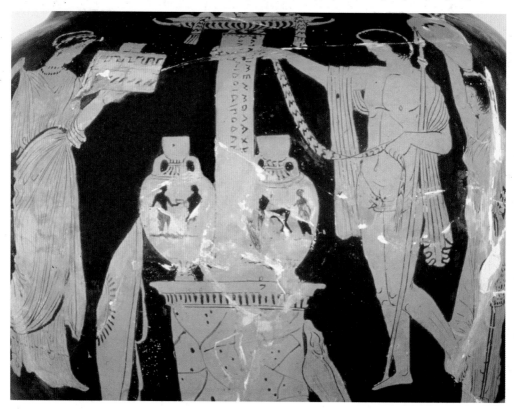

Marble statue of the Sphinx.
(540 - 530 BC, Acropolis Museum of Athens).

The Destiny of Oedipus

And so fate had it that Oedipus lived, and that he grew up to become a strong, clever young man who believed that Polybus and Merope were his parents. His real ancestry was kept a secret - until one day when, during a quarrel, someone who wanted to insult Oedipus told him that he was illegitimate and that the royal couple of Corinth were not his true parents. Unable to learn anything further from Polybus and Merope, Oedipus set out secretly to learn the truth from the Delphic oracle.

The oracle was its usual impenetrable self; but it did reveal to him that his terrible destiny would be to kill his father one day and marry his mother, and that both he and his descendants would be the source of great misfortune. Yet since nothing had been said about his ancestry, Oedipus continued to treat Polybus and Merope as his parents. Thus, to ensure that the oracle would not come true, he decided to stay away from Corinth. He set out on wanderings that took him to many places and saw him perform a multitude of feats.

Once, when he was travelling in Phocis, he came to a place where three roads met, and on the narrow road was a chariot guarded by armed men. It was none other than Laius, on his way to Delphi to find out what had happened to his son, since he was tormented by uncertainty as to whether the child had actually died. A quarrel arose when the king's men ordered the stranger to move aside to let the chariot past; Oedipus clashed with the guards and killed Laius and all his entourage - with the exception of one soldier, who managed to slip away.

Oedipus on the Throne of Thebes

At Thebes, Creon, Jocasta's brother, ruled with her after the death of Laius. But before they could begin searching for the murderer, the terror of the Sphinx engulfed the city. This monster sat on a rock at the edge of Thebes and asked passers-by a riddle and since none of them could solve it, the Sphinx devoured them. Creon announced that anyone who could solve the riddle and rid Thebes of the terrible monster would become king and marry the queen.

Oedipus, still wandering, found himself in Thebes. He was told about the Sphinx, and decided to try his luck. The riddle was as follows: "What creature of earth is it which has four legs, three legs and two legs, and is weaker the more legs it has?" Oedipus solved the problem, replying that the creature is man, who crawls on all fours as a baby, walks on two legs when he is grown, and rests on a third leg - a walking-stick - when he becomes old.

After Oedipus had solved the riddle, the Sphinx flung itself from the rock and died. As the joyful news spread, the Thebans assembled and welcomed their hero, honouring the offer of the throne. Oedipus became king, and married Jocasta. Their union produced four children: Eteocles, Polynices, Antigone and Ismene. Oedipus' reign was a peaceful one - until an epidemic broke out in the country and people began to die like flies. There seemed no way of preventing this decimation, and Oedipus, in despair, sent Creon, his wife's brother, to ask the oracle what was causing the epidemic and what could be done to save Thebes from it. The answer came back that Thebes would be saved when Laius' murderer had been driven out.

And so Oedipus himself began to investigate the affair of Laius' murder. Although things looked promising at first, he was eventually forced to enlist the help of the sooth-sayer Tiresias - who revealed that Oedipus himself was the man the oracle had meant. There could be no doubting this revelation: the word of the blind seer was accepted throughout Greece. To begin with, Oedipus had his doubts, and wondered whether the accusation might be a plot on the part of Creon. Then he thought of fleeing to Corinth, but he was held back by the oracle which had said he was to kill his father and marry his mother. But before long news came from Corinth that Polybus had died, and that the people of the city wanted Oedipus to succeed him on the throne. Yet still Oedipus was afraid that the

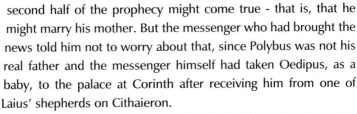

second half of the prophecy might come true - that is, that he might marry his mother. But the messenger who had brought the news told him not to worry about that, since Polybus was not his real father and the messenger himself had taken Oedipus, as a baby, to the palace at Corinth after receiving him from one of Laius' shepherds on Cithaieron.

Then the shepherd who had hidden the baby was found, and his account explained the scars which could still be seen on Oedipus' legs, proving beyond doubt what had happened. Oedipus realised that he really had killed his father and married his mother. Jocasta, filled with horror at what had been done, retired to her own rooms and hanged herself; her son (and husband) followed her indoors, took off the gold brooches from her dress and stuck their pins into his eyes, blinding himself. He begged Creon to drive him out of Thebes, imploring him also to look after Oedipus' two daughters, Antigone and Ismene. Then Oedipus came to Attica, where the kind Theseus gave him shelter. Oedipus ended his days in Attica, bringing - as yet another oracle had foretold - great good to the city where he died.

Oedipus and the Sphinx on a black-figure lekythos of 470 BC. (The Louvre, Paris).

The Sphinx of the Naxians, the famous offering at the sanctuary of Delphi made by a Naxiot sculptor. (570 BC, Archaeological Museum of Delphi).

PELOPIDES - THE FAMILY OF THE ATREIDS

Pelops and Hippodameia were the parents of Atreus, Thyestes, Pleisthenes, Pittheus (grandfather of Theseus) and Niceppe (mother of Eurystheus, uncle of Heracles). After the death of Eurystheus, who had succeeded to the throne of his father Sthenelus, the Pelopids became much more powerful and ruled in Mycenae, Tiryns, Argos and the Argolid.

According to one version of the story, Pelops passed on the sceptre of power to Atreus, his first-born.

The sons of Atreus

After their father's death, Atreus' sons Agamemnon and Menelaus took refuge in Sikyon. At some later date, Tyndareus, father of Castor and Pollux, Clytemnestra and Helen, helped Agamemnon to regain the throne which was his by right. Thyestes who reigned during that period and his son Aegisthus were exiled, and Agamemnon took Clytemnestra as his wife - after she had first killed Tantalus, her first husband, who was also a son of Thyestes. Agamemnon and Clytemnestra had three daughters - Iphigenia, Electra and Chrysothemis - and one son, Orestes. Menelaus married the beautiful Helen and ruled in Sparta.

A beautiful and pensive Helen, accompanied by a small Eros.
(Circa 410 BC, Keramikos Museum of Athens).

Poseidon emerging from the sea on a sea horse after Pelops had asked for his help.
(400 BC, hydria, Metropolitan Museum, New York).

Chapter 4

The Trojan War

The Trojan campaign was the great war that threw that far-off period into confusion. This terrible conflict lasted for ten years and cost the life of many heroes. The Achaeans and the Aeolians, Greeks from continental Greece, laid seige to and defeated the Trojans, Greeks from Asia Minor. Myth relates that the Trojan war was fought for the love of the beautiful Helen. Nevertheless, the war itself was not a myth, as was shown by the excavations of archaeologists which brought to light all the things that Homer speaks of in The Iliad.

Today the whole world knows that the Achaeans went to the coast opposite them with the full weight of their military forces to defeat fertile and civilized Troy. Moreover, there were no difficulties in making contact with and communicating as the Trojans belonged to the same race and indeed were relatives.

The Achaeans had an army of 100,00 -135,000 and a fleet of 1,186 ships. All the leaders of the Achaeans and the Aeolians took part in the campaign. The Trojans had an amazingly well-fortified town and the assistance of their own allies.

Famous Homeric heroes made their mark in this war: Achilles, the dominant figure of The Iliad, Agamemnon, Odysseus, Hector, Paris and many others. Ancient historians believed the main cause of the Trojan War was the quest for new lands, because after the descent of the Dorians in 1100 B.C., Greece was faced with threats to its survival. But the myth surrounding this war takes us back to events which are worth relating. Everything began at a wedding feast, the wedding of Peleus and Thetis.

Relief amphora from Tinos with various representations of the Trojan War. (Circa 670 BC, Archaeological Museum of Mykonos).

Modern wall painting from the Achilleio on Corfu in which Achilles is depicted on his chariot dragging the dead Hector behind him..

The Marriage of Peleus and Thetis - Achilles

P eleus was the king of Phthia, where the Myrmidons lived. He married Thetis, goddess of the sea. All the gods came to the wedding, to present their gifts and take part in the banquet. Only one divinity had been left out: Eris, goddess of controversy and discord. To avenge this slight, Eris chose her moment and tossed a golden apple in front of three of the goddesses: Hera, Athena and Aphrodite. The apple - said to have come from the garden of the Hesperides - bore an inscription: "To the most beautiful". Naturally enough, a quarrel broke out among the three goddesses, each of whom claimed the apple. Far away in the Troad, beyond the Hellespont, Paris, the young prince who was the son of king Priam, was tending his flocks.

Zeus ordered Hermes to give Paris the difficult job of judging which of the three goddesses ought to receive the golden apple, after he had weighed all the graces of each in the balance. The goddesses offered the young prince the gifts that were in their power: Hera, rule over Asia and Europe, Athena, heroism and victory - and Aphrodite, love, in the person of the comely Helen.

Paris had never seen Helen. But her reputation was so great, and his desire for love so strong, that he unhesitatingly awarded the apple to the beautiful Aphrodite. The other two goddesses were angry, and after that time supported the Achaeans against the Trojans in the war which was to ensue. Aphrodite gave Paris her advice as to how best to conquer Helen.

The union of Peleus and Thetis produced Achilles, who was destined to be the greatest of the heroes of the Trojan War. Thetis wished to make her son immortal, and so she dipped him in the waters of the sacred river Styx, holding him by the heel. As a result, he was vulnerable at that point, and the phrase "Achilles' heel" is still used today to describe someone's weak point. Peleus took his son to Chiron, the Centaur, who taught him how to hunt wild animals, the arts of war, music, painting and all the other things there were to be learned at that time.

Peleus entrusting the education of the young Achilles to the Centaur Chiron. (Circa 500 BC, black-figure lekythos, National Archaeological Museum, Athens).

Peleus abducts Thetis
while she is bathing in a spring.
(Circa 340 BC,
Etruscan krater, Rome).

The Trojans

The fortress of Troy stood on Mt. Ida, on the far side of the Hellespont. It had been built for Laomedon by Poseidon and Apollo. At the time when the events we are relating occurred, Troy was ruled by Priam, son of Laomedon, whose wife was called Hecuba. Priam had originally been named Podarces ('fine-legged'), and he was the brother of Hesione, who had followed Telamon to Salamis, married him, and borne him Teucrus and Ajax, both of whom were to fight in the Trojan War. As can be seen, the Achaeans and the Trojans were not only members of the same race, sharing a language, religion and customs, but often had family bonds, as well. Priam, ruler of the fortified city of Troy, had more children than any other ruler mentioned in the myths: fifty sons, and countless daughters. His first-born son was Hector, followed by Paris, Deiphobus, Hellen, Polydorus and Troilus; the best-known of his daughters were Creousa, Laodice, Polyxene, and Cassandra, who was gifted with the power of divination.

Priam and Hecuba, seated on their thrones, receive the sorrowful news of the murder of their son Troilus with heartfelt gestures. (Circa 540 BC, sherd of a Clazomenaean hydria, National Archaeological Museum of Athens).

Paris and Helen

As we have already seen, Agamemnon, king of Mycenae, married Clytemnestra, and Menelaus took her sister Helen. Menelaus was king in Sparta, and that was where he welcomed Paris and his entourage when they arrived bearing precious gifts. As soon as Paris set eyes on Helen, he was dazzled by her beauty. Menelaus honoured the young prince from abroad in accordance with the customs of hospitality, but on the tenth day after Paris' arrival he was forced to leave for Crete. Paris seized the opportunity to make his advances to Helen, who was unable to resist the power wielded by Aphrodite. She accepted the treasures which Paris offered her, and agreed to run away with him.

The couple escaped by night and returned to Troy, where their wedding was celebrated. But Iris, messenger to the gods, brought the news to Menelaus in Crete.

Helen and Paris.
Depicted on this Attican
red-figure lekythos is their meeting.
(End of the 5th century BC, National
Archaeological Museum of Athens).

Putting on his greaves while Thetis holds his sword and shield, Achilles prepares for his great campaign against Troy. (560 BC, black-figure tablet, National Archaeological Museum of Athens).

The Achaean Campaign Against Troy

As soon as Menelaus heard about Helen's flight he sailed from Crete and went straight to his brother Agamemnon in Mycenae. The two kings - with Nestor, the wise ruler of Pylus - decided to raise all the kings and heroes of Greece in a campaign: it was a matter of honour. The ravisher of Helen must be punished, since otherwise, if such a breach of the rules of hospitality were condoned, no one could be entirely easy in his mind about his wife.

Thus the insult which Paris offered Menelaus had to be taken as a personal affront. Odysseus, son of Laertes and king of Ithaca, was one of the men who participated in the campaign, along with Achilles, the king of Phthia, the wise Nestor, king of Pylos, Diomedes the hero of Aetolia, Ajax, the Telamonian, Ajax the Lorcian, Idas, King of Crete, the wise Palamides and Idomeneus.

The Sacrifice of Iphigenia - The Departure for Troy

A t last the fleet was ready for departure in the harbour of Aulis. But the winds were not favourable: there was dead calm, and the ships were motionless. The seer Calchas was asked to divine the cause of the lack of wind, and he replied that the goddess Artemis was angry with Agamemnon for having killed a sacred deer in a grove where she was honoured. She was determined not to allow a following wind to blow unless Agamemnon sacrificed the beautiful Iphigenia, his elder daughter, to her. To begin with, Agamemnon refused even to countenance the idea. But the troops revolted, and so a plan prepared by Odysseus was put into motion. A message was sent to the palace at Mycenae, summoning Iphigenia to Aulis, with her mother, supposedly so that she could be married to Achilles. Clytemnestra, overjoyed at her daughter's sudden good fortune, hastened to Aulis. But what she found there was an altar, and the seer ready with his knife to make the sacrifice. Everything was readied in an atmosphere of the greatest tension. But just as Calchas raised the knife, Artemis - whose unsleeping eye had been on the proceedings - bore Iphigenia off to Tauris (now the Crimea), where she became a priestess in the goddess's temple. A doe, symbolising the favour of the goddess, was sacrificed instead, to the delight of the troops. The wind immediately filled the sails of the ships, and the Greek fleet sailed out of Aulis on its way to Troy to expunge the disgrace which had been caused by Helen.

Representation of the sacrifice of Iphigenia. (370 BC, Apulian krater, British Museum, London).

A scene from of the Trojan War.
Menelaus against Paris. (The Louvre, Paris).

The Trojan War - The Iliad

Troy, otherwise known as Ilium, was a place of murderous battles, protected by Apollo with his silver bow. The first casualty of the war was Protesilaus, on the Achaean side, to whom a monument was erected and who was buried with honours. The goddesses Athena and Hera helped the Achaean forces. Homer's epic The Iliad gives a detailed account of all the events in the Trojan War, many of which had as their protagonist Achilles, a hero renowned throughout the world.

Achilles' Quarrel with Agamemnon

I t was Achilles' fate to die in Troy, which was why his mother, Thetis, had initially been so unwilling for him to take part in the war. But Agamemnon, the commander-in-chief, moved heaven and earth to have Achilles and his fearful Myrmidons by his side.

During the nine years the Trojan War lasted, Achilles captured and looted quite a number of the cities around Troy and enslaved many beautiful women, whom he presented to Agamemnon.

He kept only one slave for himself, Diomede; but she came second in Achilles' affections to Breseis, daughter of Breseus, whom he wished to marry when he returned to Phthia. Breseis, too, was a prisoner: she had been captured during a raid on the strong city of Thebes, together with another girl called Chryseida.

Chryseida was the daughter of Chryses, a priest of Apollo, and she rivalled Breseis in beauty and in the nobility of her descent. She had been promised to Agamemnon. When news came to the priest Chrysis, in the island sanctuary of Apollo where he lived, of his daughter's capture, he dressed in his sacred vestments, took rich gifts as ransom, and set off for the Greek camp to buy back his daughter.

But Agamemnon was reluctant to part with Chryseida, and so he drove Chryses away with harsh words - thus incurring the wrath of Apollo.

The arrows from the god's silver bow rained mercilessly down on the Achaean camp, spreading the plague, first among the animals and then among the men. This was the beginning of the quarrel between Achilles and Agamemnon: Achilles said that it was Agamemnon's duty to send Chryseida back to her father, so as to put an end to the plague. In the end, most reluctantly, Agamemnon let Chryseida go - but then he snatched Breseis from Achilles, in the belief that one item of booty ought to be replaced by another.

Achilles, angered by this injustice, spoke intemperately to his commander-in-chief and then withdrew to his tent, where he sat refusing to take any part in the fighting. The Trojans were delighted to see the Greeks so divided amongst themselves, and with improved morale they decimated the Achaean ranks in battle. Now that Achilles and his Myrmidons were absent, the field of battle belonged to the Trojans.

On the fringes of their military operations, Achilles and Ajax play a game with dice, similar to the present-day game of backgammon. (530 BC, black-figure amphora, Vatican Museum, Rome).

Achilles' Revenge

Achilles takes care of his wounded friend Patroclus with great skill.

I n order to plead her son's cause, Thetis climbed Olympus and begged Zeus to give her son satisfaction - after all, his life was destined to be a very short one. She implored Zeus to let the Achaeans and Agamemnon see and appreciate Achilles' worth, and also to help Achilles overcome the insult which had been done to him. But no help came to the besiegers, and Apollo with his silver bow and the arrows of Hector and the other Trojans continued to spread death among the Achaeans.

In vain Patroclus, Achilles' closest friend, begged him to do something to stop the Trojans, who seemed likely to reach the Greek ships and burn them. But Achilles was adamant. He sat in his tent all day, refusing even to consider the possibility of joining the battle. And so it came about that his beloved friend Patroclus took the initiative of leading the Myrmidons into battle himself, wearing Achilles' armour so as to mislead the Trojans.

Achilles' armour was unique: it had been made by Hephaestus himself, at the request of Thetis. When Patroclus went out to battle in Achilles' armour and with his weapons and chariot, the Trojans began in fear to retreat towards the walls of their city, believing that the king of the Myrmidons was on the battlefield once more. Patroclus succeeded in cutting off the Trojan advance before it reached the Greek camp and in striking some heavy blows against them.

Priam arrives to ask Achilles for the body of his dead son, Hector, which has been left on the ground.

But as the Trojans fell back, Apollo told Hector that the man in the armour was not really Achilles - and Hector killed Patroclus.

In his grief over the death of his friend, Achilles forgot his personal differences with Agamemnon and thought of nothing but revenge. The day after Patroclus' death, Achilles went into battle once more, scorning all the prophecies which had been made as to his imminent death.

As soon as they saw him, the Trojans turned and fled. Achilles drew closer and closer to Troy.

The Trojans mourned countless numbers of dead as the Achaean hero fought his way nearer to Hector, to revenge himself. After many battles and duels, he came upon Hector at the Scaean Gates. As the two warriors chased one another and prepared for battle, Zeus threw the fates of Achilles and Hector into the balance - and it was the destiny of Hector that dipped towards the underworld.

To pay homage to the dead Patroclus, Achilles organizes a chariot race in his friend's honour. (570 BC, sherd from a red-figure dinos, National Archaeological Museum of Athens).

And so it came about that in the duel Hector was killed. But Achilles' lust for revenge was still not quenched: he tied the corpse behind his chariot and dragged it round the city walls before returning to camp for Patroclus' funeral.

Yet when Priam came as a supplicant to his tent, to beg the body of his son for burial, Achilles greeted the aged king and father of his enemy politely.

Athena stands between the two duellists, Achilles and Hector. (The Louvre, Paris).

The Death of Achilles

The war before Troy continued. The courage and heroism of Achilles were unparalleled throughout the war. But, in the end, his death was fated to come. Achilles, at the head of his troops, had driven the Trojans back until they were at the walls of the city. Then Paris used the information which Apollo had given him and aimed his fatal arrow at the hero's only weak point: his heel. Achilles fell, and a murderous battle ensued over his body. In the end, Odysseus and Ajax managed to carry it back to the camp; at one point, Glaucus the grandson of Bellerophon attempted to drag the body off with a belt, but Ajax killed him.

Thetis and the Nereids undertook the funeral ceremonies. A magnificent tomb was built, and Achilles' ashes were placed in it, inside a gold amphora which also contained the ashes of his dearest friend, Patroclus.

Paris did not enjoy the fruits of his feat for long. Death overtook him at the hands of Philoctetes, who thus avenged the death of Achilles and the insult which the rape of Helen had meant for the Greeks.

The wounded Achilles tries to pull the fatal arrow out of his heel.
(Modern statue from the Royal Gardens of Corfu).
Opposite: The heroic figure of Achilles. (450 - 440 BC, red-figure amphora, Vatican Museum, Rome).

The Fall of Troy - The Trojan Horse

After the death of Achilles, the besiegers of Troy were forced to ponder what they could do to bring the war to a favourable conclusion. Ten years had passed, and they were beginning to despair; their courage was not what it had been. It occurred to the wily Odysseus, king of Ithaca, that the city might best be captured by a trick. So he thought up a plan, gained the consent of the other leaders, and put it into effect. A huge wooden horse was built, with a hollow stomach. When it was finished, Odysseus and eight other warriors entered the stomach of the horse through a hidden trapdoor; the horse was left outside the Greek camp in a place where it could be seen from the Trojan walls, while the remainder of the Greek forces struck camp, burned their tents and sailed off. They did not go far, however; just to the islet of Tenedus, behind which they hid from view.

The Trojans, watching the Greeks retreat, were unable to believe their eyes at first. Then they spied the wooden horse, which they approached with suspicion. It bore an inscription saying that the horse was dedicated by the Greeks to Athena. In vain Cassandra, daughter of Priam, prophesied that the horse would bring evil on the Trojans. No one was prepared to listen to her. Laocoon, priest of Apollo, hurled his javelin at the horse; it stuck in the stomach with a hollow, booming sound. He, too, tried in vain to persuade the Trojans not to trust the Achaeans. As he was speaking, the goddess Athena sent two huge serpents out of the sea, which suffocated Laocoon and his sons. The Trojans took this as a sign that the goddess would punish them if they failed to take the gift. So they towed it into the city. As soon as Troy was asleep, Odysseus and the others crept out of the wooden horse and opened the city gates. At the same time, the fleet sailed back and the Greeks launched an attack with all the force at their disposal.

They rushed in through the open gates and, by the time the Trojans had realised what was happening, it was too late. In the midst of the general massacre and destruction, Odysseus slew Priam at the altar of Zeus. The city was burned and looted - and as the flames rose, Menelaus ransacked the royal apartments of Troy in search of his wife, who had been the cause of the entire war.

As soon as Laocoon discovered that the horse was hollow,
snakes sent by Athena crushed him and his children.
(1st century BC, 'The Laocoon group',
Vatican Museum, Rome).

Menelaus furiously pursuing Helen.
(450 - 445 BC, Attican red-figure hydria, National Archaeological Museum of Athens).

When Paris was killed, Helen had married Demophobus, his brother, whom Menelaus slew that same night. Sword in hand, he rushed into Helen's rooms.

She, expecting only death from this meeting, bared her breast to accept the blow from her betrayed husband. But Menelaus' sword clattered to the floor, and husband and wife were reunited with a kiss. Menelaus took Helen away with him - and once more this fateful woman, on whose behalf a war that shook the known world had been fought, ended up as the winner of the game.

The Heroes return

I lium, as the acropolis of Troy was also known, had fallen to the cunning of Odysseus, just as the gods had decided. The surviving heroes of the war now set out on the journey home. Menelaus and Helen went back to their palace in Sparta. Agamemnon, commander-in-chief of the Greek forces, came to a bloody end. Clytemnestra, his wife, was involved in an affair with Aegisthus, his cousin. When Agamemnon returned to Mycenae, Clytemnestra killed him in his bath - and she, the faithless and murderous wife, was in turn killed with her lover Aegisthus by Orestes, son of Agamemnon and Clytemnestra. Ajax of Locris met his end in a shipwreck on the way home, while Diomedes and Idomeneus spent years in exile in southern Italy.

Very few of the heroes were able to pick up their lives where they had left off. Among those few was wise old king Nestor, who went back to Pylos and reigned in peace for the rest of his life. What, then, of the man who captured Troy, the cunning Odysseus, who could turn his hand to anything? In the end, he would come home to Ithaca, to his family and kingdom, but only after adventure upon adventure and after risking his life countless times.

The tomb of Agamemnon with Electra sitting on the steps. Orestes is shown on the left and Hermes to the right with the crown of victory. (Circa 350 BC, red-figure hydria, National Museum of Naples).

Chapter 5

The Odyssey

*A*fter Homer in The Iliad related the story
of the war that shook all of Greece
in mythical times, he went on to narrate The Odyssey.
Many experts consider this work by Homer to be more
mature containing the adventures of Odysseus,
the captor of Troy, from the time he left Troy to the moment
he reached his home in Ithaca. Odysseus,
endowed with incredible abilities, both intellectual and physical,
and imbued with the immortal spirit of the Greek race,
set off with an entire fleet to at last arrive at his longed
for island alone, exhausted and replete with experience.
During his wanderings Odysseus knew all the difficulties that
beset mariners of his day: turbulent currents and dangerous
passages, inhospitable harbours and fearsome inhabitants.
He overcame them all with his persistence and his courage
seeking out his fate and his destiny.
The people and the gods who welcomed him, loved him,
to the point they wanted to keep him there, far from
his beloved Ithaca.
His strange fate made it so he returned home alone and on a
foreign ship after starting with an entire fleet and crew.
But let us follow him on his long journey of return.

*Odysseus tied to
the mast listening to the
magical song of the Sirens.
(475 - 460 BC, stamnos,
British Museum, London).*

THE WANDERINGS OF ODYSSEUS

The cicones and the Lotus-Eaters

A fter the destruction of Troy, Odysseus set out for home with Agamemnon's fleet, but the ships were scattered in a storm. Odysseus ran aground on the coast of Thrace, where the Cicones lived. They were allies of Troy, and so Odysseus overcame and looted Ismarus, one of their cities, sparing only Maron, the priest of Apollo, who made him a gift of twelve jars of sweet intoxicating wine. The landing and the attack on the city of the Cicones cost Odysseus the lives of six men from each of his ships. Now they sailed south again, to the sea of Cythera, near Cape Maleas. Their next stop was an island off the coast of Africa. The people of the country welcomed Odysseus and his companions when they landed to reconnoitre, offering them the lotus fruit which they themselves ate. But when the sailors of the ships of Odysseus ate the fruit they forgot their homelands and their wish to return there. In the end, Odysseus had to use force to get them to re-embark.

In the country of the Cyclopses

O dysseys' little fleet now sailed north and anchored at an island in the land of the Cyclopses, which in all likelihood was Sicily. When they landed, Odysseus took with him twelve of his companions and goatskins of the wine of Maron as a gift to any people they might meet. On their way they came to a cave which contained huge quantities of fresh milk and cheese. Odysseus was so curious about the enormous objects there that he paid no heed to his companions, who wanted to leave; he wanted to see for himself just how enormous the being was who lived there. When the owner of the cave, the Cyclops Polyphemus, came home he saw the strangers and imprisoned them in the cave by blocking its mouth with a boulder so large fifty men could not have moved it. He immediately devoured two of Odysseus' companions and then continued to eat them in pairs. Odysseus offered him some of the sweet wine of Maron. Polyphemus drank a good deal and in his merry mood he asked Odysseus what his name was. "My name is Noman" came the hero's reply. To repay Odysseus for his fine gift, the Cyclops promised to eat him last.

Odysseus did not know how he was going to escape from this cannibalistic monster. In the beginning he thought of killing him. But how would they remove the stone from the mouth of the cave? So he decided to blind him. Drunk, the Cyclops had fallen into a deep sleep. Using a pointed stick they found, they heated it in the fire and drove it into the Cyclops' solitary eye. The cries of Polyphemus in the night shook the island. The other Cyclopses hastened over asking the name of the person who blinded him. But when the giant replied "Noman" they thought he had gone mad and returned to their caves since "no man" had hurt him. In the morning, Polyphemus searched in vain for those who had injured him. Odysseus and his companions escaped from the cave by clinging to the bellies of the sheep. After he had raised the sails and pulled away from the island Odysseus called out to Polyphemus that if he were ever asked who had blinded him, he should answer, "Odysseus, the conqueror of Troy". In a rage the Cyclops sought revenge from his father Poseidon. This was the beginning of the almighty god of the sea's wrath over Odysseus and the start of a new round of troubles.

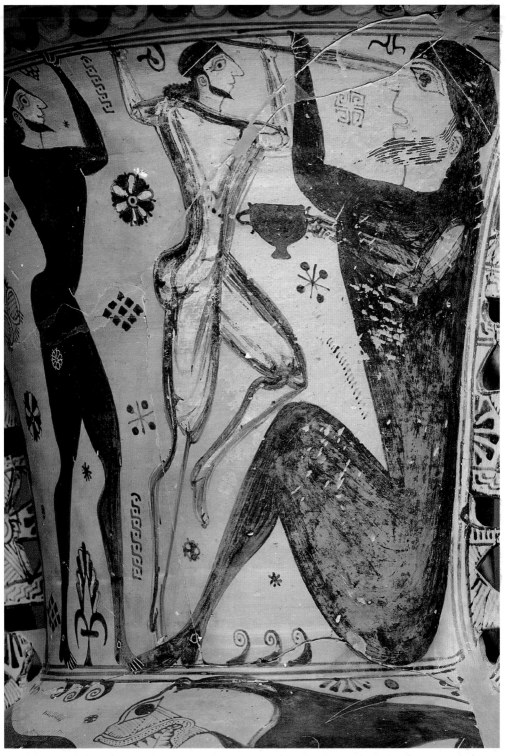

Odysseus manages, through ingenuity and resolve, to hammer the pole into the eye of the Cyclops, Polyphemus.
(Circa 670 BC, Early Attican krater, Archaeological Museum of Eleusis).

On the Island of Aelus

Odysseus' companions disobey
his orders and one of them opens
the oxhide bag of Aeolus.
*The first wind emerges menacingly
from the mouth of the bag.
(End of the 5th century BC,
Etruscan art cameo).*

The next stop after the country of Polyphemus was the island of Aeolus, master of the winds. Aeolus made Odysseus and his companions welcome, and offered them hospitality for a month. When the time came for them to leave, he presented Odysseus with a priceless gift: a bag made of ox-leather in which he had shut up all the strong winds. Only one wind had been left free: the breeze Zephyr, which would blow gently and take the ships straight home to Ithaca. Odysseus passed on to his companions Aeolus' warning that the bag was not to be opened because the winds would escape and blow them into great dangers on the rest of their voyage. But the crew did not obey their master. They thought Aeolus had given Odysseus a bag of rare wine - and so when Odysseus was asleep one night someone opened the bag. Out rushed the howling winds. The little ship spun round and round like a nutshell in the fearsome storm. The gale blew them back to the island of Aeolus, but it was in vain that Odysseus begged Aeolus to send them another tail-wind; he was convinced now that the gods did not want to help Odysseus, so he left him to his fate.

The Island of Circe

Sailing on now as the winds might take them, Odysseus and his crew reached the country of the Laestrygonians, who were fierce eaters of human flesh. They escaped by the skin of their teeth from the cannibals, who pursued them with stones and sank all but one of their ships. This last craft and its crew were all that Odysseus had left when he sailed north again, to the island of Circe.

To begin with, Circe welcomed the detachment which Odysseus sent out to reconnoitre under Eurylochus. But after serving them a banquet she began to touch them with her magic wand and turn them into swine and other animals. Eurylochus managed to escape and brought news to Odysseus of what was happening. He decided to go to meet the witch, to persuade her to give his sailors their human form once more. At first, Circe tried the same trick on Odysseus, but he proved invulnerable to her charms - thanks to a magic potion which Hermes had given him before he approached the palace. Odysseus threatened Circe with his sword and extracted from her a promise, under oath, that she would harm none of the company. The rest of their stay on the island was pleasant. During it, on Circe's advice, Odysseus descended into the underworld to ask the soul of Tiresias, the seer, about his return home. Tiresias told him he would have to go home alone, on a strange ship, and that he would be avenged on the suitors who wished to marry his wife.

The sorceress Circe offers wine to Odysseus' companions.
(480 - 470 BC, Attican black-figure lekythos, National Archaeological Museum of Athens).

The Island of the Sirens

The Sirens, whom we have met before - in the story of the Argonauts - were the next threat in store on Odysseus' voyage. In order to prevent his sailors from being overcome by the song of these evil spirits, who were half-women and half-birds, the wily Odysseus blocked up his companions' ears with wax. But he himself was curious to hear what the song of the Sirens sounded like. So he ordered the crew to lash him to the mast of the ship, where he could listen without endangering anyone. He told the sailors that if he should attempt to tell them in sign language to set him free, they were to bind him still tighter. And so matters fell out.

Left: Odysseus, bound, listens to the music of the Sirens. (Circa 500 BC, black-figure lekythos, National Archaeological Musuem of Athens).

Bottom: An Etruscan relief showing Odysseus with his companions passing the island of the Sirens. (2nd century BC, the Louvre, Paris).

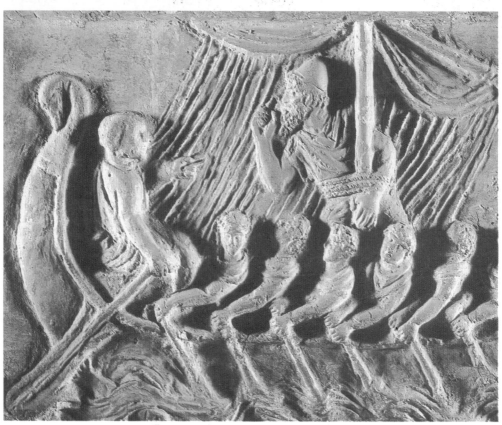

A 5th century BC relief found on Milos which depicts Scylla. (British Museum, London).

Scylla and Charybdis

After passing the island of the magical Sirens, Odysseus next had to deal with the Clashing Rocks and the channel between Scylla and Charybdis. Scylla was a sea monster which resembled a woman from the waist up, the remainder being composed of six fierce, monstrous dogs. She lived in a cave on the Italian side of the Strait of Messina, and she devoured passing sailors.

Just opposite, on the other side of the strait which separates Italy from Sicily, was Charybdis. This gigantic monster swallowed vast quantities of sea water three times a day, sweeping down her throat anything which happened to be floating past on the sea, including ships. Then she regurgitated the water she had swallowed.

These monsters made the Strait of Messina an extremely dangerous place, because it was not possible to avoid both of them. In the end, Odysseus sailed closer to Scylla so as not to be swallowed by Charybdis, and she devoured some of his sailors.

The Oxen of the Sun - The Island of Calypso

The island of Thrinacia was Odysseus' next stop. Here there were herds of white oxen sacred to the Sun. The winds prevented the companions from sailing on and their supplies had run out. Odysseus had strictly forbidden the sailors to slaughter and eat the sacred oxen of the Sun, but they disobeyed him and, in their hunger, killed and roasted some.

Helios, the sun god, demanded that Zeus punish Odysseus for this insult. As soon as the companions set out on their voyage once more, their ship ran into a storm, was struck by one of Zeus' thunderbolts, and sank. Only Odysseus, who had refused to eat any of the meat of the sacred oxen, was saved and washed up on the shores of Ogygia, the island of Calypso. It was thus as a castaway that Calypso found him. She was a nymph, the daughter of Atlas, and she lived in a deep and beautifully decorated cave which led out into wonderful gardens and forests. Odysseus spent an enchanted time with Calypso. She did everything in her power to keep him by her - even going so far as to promise him immortality. But his desire to go home would not fade in his heart; and one day Zeus, on the request of Athena, sent Hermes to beg Calypso to let Odysseus go home at last. Calypso even helped Odysseus find the wood he needed to make a raft, and provided him with supplies and advice for the journey.

On the Island of the Phaeacians

Calypso sadly bade Odysseus farewell, and he set off in an easterly direction. But the wrath of Poseidon had not yet died away. He blew up mountainous waves, wrecked Odysseus' raft, and cast him into the sea once more. After hours of struggle with death among the wreckage of his raft, Odysseus was washed ashore, exhausted, on the island of the Phaeacians, now called Corfu (but which Homer terms Scheria).

In his exhaustion, he fell asleep, but was wakened by girlish voices. It was Nausicaa, daughter of king Alcinous and queen Arete, rulers of the island, with the maidens of the palace. The girls had come to a nearby stream to wash clothes. When Nausicaa saw the stranger, she helped him up, gave him clothes to wear and showed him the way to her father's palace.

Alcinous and Arete welcomed Odysseus very warmly he told them of all his adventures and hardships. They expressed their sympathy, their admiration of his feats, which had made him famous everywhere, and their desire that he should stay with them and marry Nausica. But Odysseus politely explained that he was longing for his home, Ithaca, and when they heard that, the king and queen were so moved that they lent him a ship to take him to Ithaca. On the way, Odysseus fell asleep.

The Phaeacians set him ashore on a quiet beach on Ithaca, surrounded by the gifts of Alcinous. The time set by the gods had come for Odysseus to set foot on his home island, after an absence of twenty years.

Odysseus, under the protective gaze of Athena and holding branches of supplication, approaches Nausicaa, the daughter of king Alcinous.

Odysseus in Ithaca

When he realised he had reached Ithaca, Odysseus went first to the hut of Eumaeus, his swineherd, in whom he had complete trust. Once Eumeaus had recognised him, Odysseus met Telemachus and learned about what had been happening at the palace.

The suitors who wished to marry Penelope - and thus ascend the throne - had gathered from all over Ithaca and the other lands over which Odysseus held sway. They had installed themselves in the palace, eating and drinking at Odysseus' expense and squandering his fortune. Penelope had initially been able to keep them at bay by a trick, telling them that she would make her choice as soon as she had finished weaving a shroud for her father-in-law, old Laertes, which she was making on her loom. Penelope wove all day - but at night, in secret, she undid what she had woven. In the end, the secret got out, and now eight of the suitors were becoming more insistent and the queen had been forced into a corner. She was under pressure from all sides to make up her mind as to which suitor she would marry. When Odysseus found out about all this, he decided to teach them a lesson they would never forget. He disguised himself as a beggar and entered the palace with Telemachus. No one recognised him, except Argus, his faithful dog, who had been merely a puppy when Odysseus set off for Troy. As soon as he saw his master, Argus climbed to his feet, lay down in front of Odysseus, wagged his tail, and died.

A depiction showing the old woman Eurycleia recognizing Odysseus from the broad scar on his leg while Eumaeus, who led Odysseus to the palace, now offers him a gift. (Circa. 440 BC, red-figure skyphos).

Right: Penelope sits sadly before her loom whilst her son, Telemachus, looks at her thoughtfully.

Odysseus Takes Revenge on the Suitors

The sudden appearance of this unknown beggar, asking for food, caused the suitors to behave roughly towards him. When she was told that a stranger had turned up, Penelope was the only person who wanted to talk to him - in case he had some news of her husband. Odysseus did not reveal himself to her, but he raised her hopes that Odysseus would be coming soon. Penelope, however, was unwilling to believe him, and so she announced that the suitors would compete against each other in games. She would marry the winner. The archery contest required considerable skill on the part of the competitors - not least because first they had to bend the bow of Odysseus himself, which Penelope had kept safe. Then they had to shoot the arrow through the holes in a number of axes set in a line. One after another the suitors tried, but they all failed even to bend the bow. In the end, Odysseus asked if he could try. With amazement, the suitors saw him bend the bow easily and hit the target effortlessly with his first shot. The hour of reckoning had come. Odysseus' devoted servants locked all the palace doors and the king and his son Telemachus picked up the weapons which they had left earlier in an upper room. The slaughter of the suitors followed. Word came to Penelope in her apartments, and she hardly dared believe that her husband had come home. In the end, he convinced her of his identity by revealing secrets that only the two of them knew, and by describing her bridal chamber.

Epilogue

On the following day, Odysseus looked round his farms. Now it was time for old Laertes to feel the joy of locking his son in his arms and recognising him. However, the families of the suitors now gathered in an armed mob seeking vengeance for the massacre of their sons. The goddess Athena disguised herself as sweet- spoken, wise old mentor, and acted as the intermediary to calm everyone down and ensure that peace and good order reigned in Ithaca.

That is the story of Odysseus as told by Homer in his Odyssey, generally regarded as the oldest and most reliable version of the narrative. Odysseus is the eternal Greek, with his passions, his weaknesses, his guile, his cunning, his wit and his in-ventiveness.

He is a mortal, everyday figure with his feet placed firmly on the ground.

He is anyone at all, anywhere on earth - anyone going forward for the sake of the journey, to reach his journey's end, his Ithaca.

Homer *was the greatest poet of all time.*
We know little of his life, not even precisely where he came from.
Seven towns have vied for the honor: Smyrna, Rhodes, Colophon,
Salamis on Cyprus, Chios, Argos and Athens.
Smyrna is considered the most likely
as there are many Ionian elements in his work,
The poet lived during the 9th century B.C. His immortal epics,
The Iliad and The Odyssey are the oldest and finest works of literature
in the world while many others are also attributed to him.
A number of writers believe he lived at the time of the Trojan War
while others maintain he came after it.
Homer died on the island of Ios and was buried there like a hero
with sacrifices and dedications in his honor.
The detailed descriptions in his work of the life and the culture
of the Greeks during his period, are the golden legacy of Greece
to the rest of the world.

One final word

We hope that in this brief work we have managed
to present both a concise and yet comprehensive picture of Greek
Mythology. Myths whether religious, historical or didactic,
and beyond any truth they may contain, show us the development
of human thought. In its entirety mythology is an inexhaustible
source from which can be drawn material for endless texts.
Many of the figures we mention simply as names
in the various chapters and sections have their own myth,
perhaps less well-known but nevertheless interesting and unique.
Here it should be stressed that there are a number of versions
of the same myth depending on the area in which each thrived.
We selected the best known of these variations which are also the ones
that have prevailed. What is of particular interest here is that in
the total number of narrations, there are many events that
do not have a logical place in time. Myths referring to the same subject
and which have survived separately speak of the same matters
and yet they appear to have taken place at different times.
Heroes, for example, live the events of one period, while in another
text it is related that these events were acted out during a time
when the heroes themselves were elsewhere.
So, we must accept that myths have a very flexible time frame.
Furthermore, our far-off ancestors when they were making their world
and taking their first important steps in the evolution of mankind,
had no idea that we would all be so involved with these experiences
so many years later. Otherwise - who can say? - they might have tried
to fill in all the empty spaces they left, against their will, for the students
of today who are trying to find the truth in the so distant past.
But what remains of unquestioned importance is the fact that
from those distant centuries have survived written testimony,
objects and above all else works of rare art which prove the existence
of everything we have set forth.
Whether you come across them in Greece, their homeland,
or in the great museums of the world, ask them.
They have so much to tell you!

Bibliography

*Our sources for this brief and yet,
we hope, comprehensive presentation,
are taken from ancient Greek literature and a number
of eminent writers from that time are mentioned in our text:
Hesiod, Homer, Apollodorus,
Apollonius of Rhodes, Strabo, Plutarch,
Pausanias, Pindar, Theocritus, Euripides, Sophocles,
Aeschylus, and Lucian to name but a few.
We took valuable information and analyses from the modern studies
of K. Kerenoi, I. Karkides, Rispen and Pierre Grimal.
This book is not designed to fill a specific
gap in international bibliography and should not be judged
on such a basis. There are many Greek and foreign experts
who have already done honour to this area.
This book aims for simplicity and cogency in its treatment of the
subjects of Greek mythology, full of love and respect for its sources.
We feel that Greek mythology is of universal value
and that is why people everywhere should
become famillar with it.*

Index